API-ocalypse Now: Python's Guide to Secure and Flexible Data Handling

Survive the API Jungle with Python's Most Powerful Tools for Security and Flexibility

By Paddy Donohue

Dedication

To my wife Cyndy and daughter Shannon—who have patiently endured countless hours of debugging sessions, software updates, and impromptu tech lectures. Without your support, this book might have been finished much sooner, but certainly with fewer coffee breaks. Thank you!

About the Author

With over three decades of experience in the wild jungles of information technology, **Paddy** has been at the forefront of application development and API engineering, armed with little more than a keyboard, a dry sense of humor, and an uncanny ability to debug anything thrown his way. From mastering Python's intricacies to taming SQLAlchemy, Paddy has built scalable, secure, and downright impressive solutions that would make even the most seasoned developer stop and say, "How did you do that?"

A proud introvert with a preference for the quiet life of freelance work, Paddy has honed his ability to tackle the toughest programming problems with minimal fanfare. His dedication to continuous learning, particularly in cybersecurity, keeps him sharp and ready to fend off any rogue SQL injection or errant cross-site scripting attack.

When he's not wrangling APIs or waxing poetic about the virtues of FastAPI, Paddy is likely experimenting with the latest tech trends, finding elegant solutions to complex problems, or fine-tuning his DIY home server setup (because, let's face it, why rent cloud servers when you can build your own?). His passion for technology is matched only by his dedication to family and his insistence that every piece of code should be both functional and beautiful—kind of like a perfectly brewed cup of coffee.

This book, **API-ocalypse Now**, is his debut as an author, blending his deep technical expertise with his signature dry wit. It's a guide for developers, from novices to seasoned pros, looking to survive and thrive in the ever-evolving world of APIs.

Table of Contents

Dedication..2
About the Author...3
Foreword...5
Preface..6
Acknowledgments..7
Introduction: Welcome to the API Jungle...............................8
Chapter 1: FastAPI and Friends – The Dream Team for APIs.............10
Chapter 2: The First Steps – Setting Up FastAPI..................16
Chapter 3: Data Modeling with Pydantic – No More Wild Inputs........21
Chapter 4: Storing and Retrieving Data – The SQLAlchemy Way.......29
Chapter 5: Bringing It All Together – Building a Full-Stack Front-End with Jinja2...36
Chapter 6: CRUD – The Backbone of Every API (and Our Jungle).....44
Chapter 7: Securing Your API – Fortifying Your Jungle Camp............49
Chapter 8: Mastering FastAPI's /docs – Your Built-In Testing Ground 60
Chapter 9: Performance Tuning and Scalability – Taming the API Jungle...73
Chapter 10: Automated Function Testing – Keep the Jungle Running Smoothly..83
Chapter 11: Securing Your API – Beyond the Basics...........90
Chapter 12: API Documentation Best Practices...................97
Chapter 13: Deploying Your API – From Local to Cloud..................105
Chapter 14: Monitoring and Observability in FastAPI......................111
Chapter 15: Real-Time Features with WebSockets..............118
Chapter 16: Creating a Front-end for Your API.................125
Chapter 17: API Versioning and Evolution........................132
Chapter 18: Performance Benchmarks and Tuning............139
Chapter 19: Building a Python Tool for API Testing.........147
Bibliography..152
Notes:...154

Foreword

APIs are the arteries of modern software development, quietly powering everything from the apps on our phones to the vast systems of automation that keep entire industries running. I've spent years in the trenches of application development, witnessing first-hand how crucial well-built, secure, and scalable APIs are for developers.

This book is not just another how-to manual. It's a field guide, designed to help you navigate the dense, ever-changing world of API development. Whether you're new to APIs or have been building them for years, my hope is that this book will give you the practical insights and hard-won lessons you need to create fast, secure, and flexible APIs.

Welcome to the jungle. Now, let's build.

Preface

The idea for this book came to me during one of those long coding sessions where the coffee is endless, and the bugs are even more so. As I worked through yet another API integration, I realized that while there were countless resources out there, few of them spoke to the developer in me—someone who wanted clear, practical guidance mixed with a bit of humor to keep things from getting too dry.

FastAPI, in particular, was a breath of fresh air. It's fast, it's modern, and it makes building APIs so much easier. But, like anything in software, there's a learning curve, and I wanted to flatten that curve for developers by creating a resource that's as fun to read as it is informative.

This book is the culmination of decades of coding, debugging, and learning, often the hard way. My goal is to save you a few late nights and give you the tools to build better, faster, and more secure APIs.

For those looking to follow along with the examples or explore the code in more detail, I've made source code available at: https://github.com/Paddy-Wa/API-ocalypse-Now-source.

Acknowledgments

No book is written in isolation, and this one is no exception. I'd like to thank my family for tolerating my endless coding marathons and for always knowing when to bring more coffee. Special thanks go to my colleagues, mentors, and the vibrant FastAPI community—your shared knowledge and passion helped shape this book in ways I couldn't have done alone.

A big shoutout to TryHackMe.com and HackTheBox.com for providing countless hours of learning and challenges that kept my mind sharp, my skills honed, and my sense of fun alive. Your platforms have been indispensable in my ongoing education and have undoubtedly influenced my approach to API security.

Thanks also to the readers and developers who keep pushing the boundaries of what APIs can do. You've made this journey worthwhile.

Introduction: Welcome to the API Jungle

The world of APIs is a lot like the jungle—dense, full of hidden dangers, and, at times, a little intimidating. But for those willing to hack their way through the thicket, it's incredibly rewarding. You're here because you want to survive this API jungle and, maybe, even thrive in it. Well, grab your machete (or in this case, your favorite IDE), and let's trek into Python's untamed wilderness together.

In this guide, we'll be your trusty jungle guides, walking you step-by-step through the creation of secure, flexible APIs using Python and some of its most powerful tools: **FastAPI, SQLAlchemy, Pydantic, SQLite,** and **FastAPI_Simple_Security**. Whether you're new to APIs or have been wrestling with them for years, this book will equip you with everything you need to build fast, secure, and scalable APIs—without getting eaten alive by the competition.

APIs are the connective tissue of the web—providing a way for applications to talk to each other, share data, and get things done. Think of them like a jungle ecosystem, where each species interacts with others in ways that keep everything functioning smoothly. But just like in the jungle, things can get a little wild if you don't know what you're doing. One wrong step, and you might fall into a pit of security vulnerabilities, performance bottlenecks, or tangled data.

But here's the good news: you're not alone in this journey. You've got Python by your side—the ultimate Swiss Army knife for the modern developer. With the tools we'll introduce, you'll not only survive the API jungle, but you'll also learn to thrive in it, building APIs that are secure, fast, and scalable, all while having a bit of fun along the way. After all, if you can't laugh while debugging, you're doing it wrong.

Along the way, we'll encounter wild creatures (like asynchronous requests), hidden traps (poor security practices), and tangled vines (messy data). But don't worry—with Python and a strong cup of coffee in hand, you'll have all the tools you need to hack your way through and build something powerful, maintainable, and downright fun to work with.

By the end of this book, you won't just be a survivor of the API jungle—you'll be its master. Whether it's navigating asynchronous programming, crafting Pydantic models, optimizing SQLAlchemy queries, or securing your API with JWT tokens, you'll have the skills to tackle it all. You'll be able to confidently create APIs that stand the test of time—and the relentless demands of modern development.

To help you follow along, source code for this book is available at the official repository: https://github.com/Paddy-Wa/API-ocalypse-Now-source. You can clone the repository and build the projects step-by-step.

So, let's dive in, shall we? The jungle awaits.

Chapter 1: FastAPI and Friends – The Dream Team for APIs

FastAPI is like that one friend who shows up to a project and gets everything done twice as fast as you expected, and does it all with a smile. It's modern, high-performance, and designed specifically for building APIs. Compared to its peers—Flask, Django, and even more seasoned veterans—FastAPI is the rising star, the newcomer that's taking over the API world one async request at a time.

But why FastAPI? Well, let's start with its core feature: **speed**. It's called FastAPI for a reason—it's asynchronous, built on Python 3's ASGI (Asynchronous Server Gateway Interface), and it's fast. Very fast. In fact, some benchmarks show it can handle requests as quickly as Node.js or Go, which are notorious for their speed.

FastAPI also comes with built-in support for **OpenAPI** and **JSON Schema**, making it perfect for documenting and sharing your APIs right out of the box. No more extra work to generate docs or explain your API to others—it's all there, ready to go. It's like having an instruction manual show up with your IKEA furniture. And it's actually useful.

The Rise of FastAPI: Popularity Over Time Compared to Flask and Django

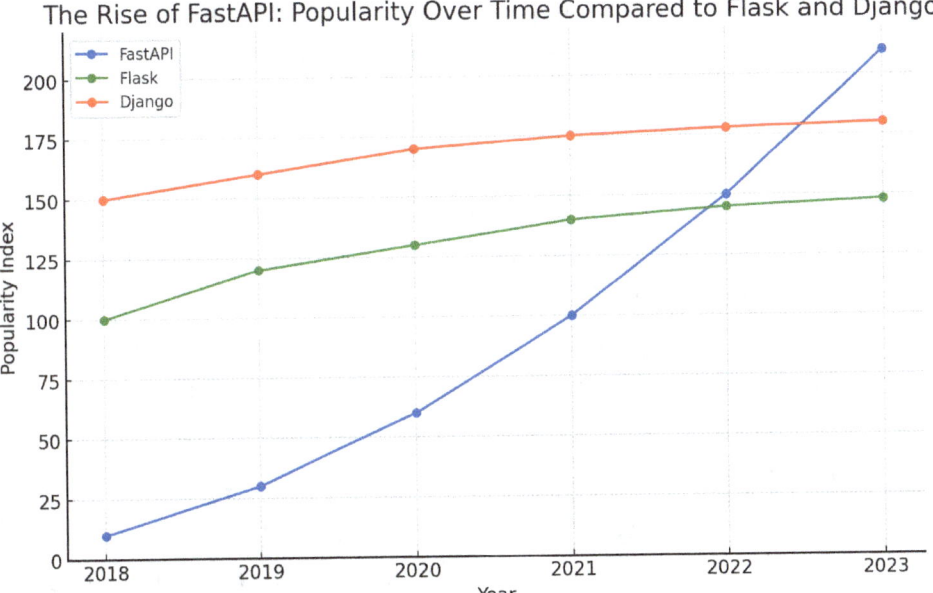

Comparison: Let's compare FastAPI to some of its peers:

- **Flask**: Flask is a great, lightweight framework, but you'll need to roll out your own authentication and async support. Imagine showing up to a jungle expedition with only a Swiss Army knife.
- **Django**: Django is the heavyweight champ. It's got everything—authentication, a templating engine, and an ORM—but it's heavy. It's the equivalent of bringing a full kitchen setup when you only needed a camp stove.
- **FastAPI**: Enter FastAPI—light, fast, and async. It brings the essentials to the API table, but does it without all the overhead. It's perfect for modern, microservice-based applications where speed and security matter.

FastAPI also pairs perfectly with **SQLAlchemy** (for database ORM) and **Pydantic** (for data validation). These two are the peanut butter and jelly of the Python world—tasty on their own but even better together. SQLAlchemy handles the database interactions while Pydantic makes sure your data is clean and validated.

Key Libraries

- **FastAPI**: The rising star of Python frameworks, FastAPI is designed for building APIs quickly, efficiently, and with minimal code. It's asynchronous by nature, making it ideal for handling many requests simultaneously. With built-in support for OpenAPI, FastAPI provides automatic documentation, making development and integration a breeze.

- **SQLAlchemy**: SQLAlchemy is Python's go-to Object Relational Mapper (ORM) for interacting with databases. It abstracts the complexities of database queries and connections while offering full control when needed. You'll be using it to connect, manage, and query your database, whether it's SQLite, MySQL, or PostgreSQL.

- **Pydantic**: Pydantic is all about data validation. It allows you to define models and automatically validate incoming data, ensuring that your API only processes valid and structured inputs. With Pydantic, you can catch bad data before it wreaks havoc in your system.

- **Jinja2**: Jinja2 is a templating engine that lets you create dynamic HTML pages. While FastAPI is primarily a back-end framework, Jinja2 gives you the power to render server-side HTML templates when building full-stack applications.

- **Security (JWT)**: JSON Web Tokens (JWT) are a modern standard for securing APIs. JWTs are compact, secure, and easy to implement, providing a stateless way to authenticate and authorize users across distributed systems.

MVC Code Separation

To ensure our code remains organized and easy to maintain, we'll follow an **MVC-like** structure, keeping our database and model logic separate. Specifically, we'll place the database connection logic in `db.py` and the model definitions in `model.py`.

- **db.py**: Handles the database connection and session creation. This file will define how our API interacts with the database, ensuring a clean separation of concerns.

- **model.py**: Contains the data models (e.g. SQLAlchemy models) that represent the structure of our database. Keeping this separate ensures that our models are easy to modify and extend without touching the rest of the application.

In future chapters, we'll provide instructions for creating a directory structure that supports this separation of concerns, ensuring a scalable and maintainable API.

Why FastAPI is Winning the Race

So why is FastAPI taking the developer world by storm? It's not just luck or a cool name—it's because it solves real problems, and it does so with style. Here's why it's growing so fast:

- **Ease of Use**: FastAPI is incredibly intuitive. You can build APIs with minimal code, and yet it's flexible enough for large projects. It feels like Python should feel: fast, clean, and to the point.

- **Asynchronous by Nature**: Unlike some of the older frameworks, FastAPI was built with modern web apps in mind. It supports async out of the box, meaning it can handle lots of requests simultaneously—perfect for today's high-performance apps.

- **Built-in Documentation**: FastAPI generates **OpenAPI docs** for you. You don't need to waste time building documentation manually—it's like having an API translator that makes your code instantly understandable to other developers.

- **Performance**: FastAPI is fast. Really fast. And in the API world, speed is everything. It rivals the performance of Node.js and Go, but with the elegance of Python.

Project Overview: What You'll Build

By the end of this book, you'll have built a fully functioning, secure API from scratch. Here's a sneak peek at what you'll be building:

- A **FastAPI-based API** that serves dynamic routes.
- A **relational database** using SQLAlchemy, managing records like a pro.
- A **user authentication system** powered by JWT (JSON Web Tokens) for secure login and token-based authorization.
- **Dynamic HTML pages** rendered with Jinja2 (because who doesn't love a little full-stack development?).

In other words, you'll go from API explorer to API **safari guide**, navigating through the jungle of web development with ease!

Common API Pitfalls (and How FastAPI Saves the Day)

Building APIs can be tricky. Here are some common pitfalls developers face—and how FastAPI helps you avoid them:

1. **Bad Documentation**: Ever had to use an API with no docs, or worse, outdated ones? FastAPI automatically generates OpenAPI docs, so you're always in sync.

2. **Slow Performance**: Handling lots of requests can bog down your API. With its async capabilities, FastAPI can handle multiple requests concurrently, keeping things smooth and fast.

3. **Data Validation Woes**: Incorrect or missing data can break your API. With **Pydantic**, FastAPI automatically validates incoming data, ensuring your API doesn't crash from bad inputs.

4. **Security Flaws**: Securing an API isn't easy. FastAPI makes it easier by supporting JWT authentication right out of the box, so you can focus on building features, not fending off hackers.

Chapter 2: The First Steps – Setting Up FastAPI

Building an API is like putting together a puzzle. You need to start with the right pieces. Before we dive into coding, let's get our environment set up. If you're already familiar with Python environments, feel free to skip ahead. If not, don't worry—this will be as painless as setting up a tent in the jungle (which is to say, only slightly frustrating).

Setting Up a Python Virtual Environment

Before anything else, you need to isolate your project's dependencies. This is where **virtual environments** come into play. They allow you to create a sandboxed environment, ensuring that the Python packages you install for this project won't conflict with other projects on your machine.

Here's how you create and activate a virtual environment on different platforms:

- **For macOS/Linux**:

```
$ python3 -m venv venv
$ source venv/bin/activate
```

- **For Windows**:

```
$ python -m venv venv
$ .\venv\Scripts\activate
```

Once your virtual environment is activated, you can install dependencies specific to this project without affecting the global Python installation.

Managing Dependencies with `pip` and `requirements.txt`

Now that we've set up our virtual environment, it's time to manage dependencies. You'll need **FastAPI**, **Uvicorn** (the ASGI server that runs your FastAPI app), and **SQLAlchemy** for database management.

To install these, run the following commands in your terminal:

```
pip install fastapi uvicorn sqlalchemy
```

After installing the packages, you can create a `requirements.txt` file to track your dependencies:

```
pip freeze > requirements.txt
```

This file lists all the packages installed in your virtual environment, making it easy to share your project with others or redeploy it later. To reinstall the same packages later, simply run:

```
pip install -r requirements.txt
```

Environment-Specific Configurations with `.env`

Next, let's prepare your FastAPI project structure. Before we get started with writing the API logic, let's organize our files. Create the following structure:

```
project/
├── main.py          # FastAPI app entry point
├── db.py            # Database connection logic
├── .env             # Environment variables
└── requirements.txt # List of dependencies
```

- **main.py**: This will be the entry point of our FastAPI app.
- **db.py**: We'll put database connection logic here.
- **.env**: This file will store sensitive data like database URLs and secret keys.

Here's an example `.env` file:

```
# .env
DATABASE_URL=sqlite:///./test.db
SECRET_KEY=mysecretkey
```

To load these values into your FastAPI app, you'll add the following code to `main.py`:

```python
# main.py
from fastapi import FastAPI
from dotenv import load_dotenv
import os
import uvicorn

load_dotenv()
DATABASE_URL = os.getenv("DATABASE_URL")
SECRET_KEY = os.getenv("SECRET_KEY")

app = FastAPI()

@app.get("/")
async def index():
    return {"message": "Welcome to the API Jungle Baby!"}

if __name__ == "__main__":
```

```
uvicorn.run("main:app", port=8080, reload=True)
```

Setting Up Unit Testing

Testing is an important part of any project, and although we'll dive deeper into it in later chapters, it's a good idea to set up the groundwork now. **Unit tests** help ensure that each part of your API behaves as expected.

To get started, let's organize the project structure:

```
project/
├── main.py          # FastAPI app entry point
├── db.py            # Database connection logic
├── .env             # Environment variables
├── tests/           # Directory for all test files
│   └── __init__.py  # empty file treats dirs as mods
│   └── test_main.py # Your first unit test
└── requirements.txt # List of dependencies
```

Once the structure is ready, install **pytest** for testing:

```
pip install pytest httpx python-dotenv
```

We'll use `pytest` to run unit tests, and FastAPI's `TestClient` will allow us to send HTTP requests to the API routes during testing.

Now, in `test_main.py`, let's set up a simple test for the root endpoint of your FastAPI app:

```python
# test/test_main.py
from fastapi.testclient import TestClient
from main import app  # Import your FastAPI app

client = TestClient(app)

def test_read_root():
    response = client.get("/")
    assert response.status_code == 200
    assert response.json() == {"message": "Welcome to the API Jungle"}
```

This test uses FastAPI's **TestClient** to simulate a GET request to the root endpoint (/) and checks that the response has a status code of 200 and contains the expected JSON message.

Why Start Testing Now?

Even though we're just setting up, introducing testing early in the process is crucial. It helps ensure that as we add more features to our API, we can continuously verify that everything is working as intended without having to manually test each route.

As we build out the API, we'll dive deeper into testing strategies in later chapters, where we'll cover:

- Writing tests for specific API routes.
- Validating input and output data.
- Mocking external services during testing.

For now, this setup ensures you're ready to test as we add more functionality to the API.

Chapter 3: Data Modeling with Pydantic – No More Wild Inputs

So, you've set up your FastAPI app and organized your files. Now, it's time to handle the data flowing into your API. But before data gets anywhere near your business logic or database, you need to make sure it's valid. This is where **Pydantic** shines—helping you ensure that all the data coming into your API is clean, structured, and ready to use.

Separating Models into `model.py`

As part of our **MVC-like structure**, it's a best practice to separate your data models from your main application logic. We'll store our data models in a `model.py` file, making it easier to keep track of and manage as your API grows.

Using Pydantic for Data Validation

Pydantic is an incredibly powerful tool for defining and validating the data models that your API will use. Think of it as a bouncer for your API—it checks every piece of data that comes in, and if something doesn't meet your requirements, it doesn't let it through the door.

Let's start with a simple model to represent an **Animal** in our API. We'll store this model in `model.py`:

```python
from pydantic import BaseModel, conint

class Animal(BaseModel):
    name: str
    species: str
    age: conint(ge=0)  # Age must be a non-negative integer
```

Here, we're using `conint(ge=0)` to ensure that the animal's age is a non-negative integer. But Pydantic's validation powers go way beyond this simple case. Let's explore some other ways we can validate incoming data.

Ways to Validate Data with Pydantic

1. Constrained Types (constr, conint, conlist)

Pydantic allows you to use **constrained types** to impose specific conditions on your data. Here are a few examples:

- `constr`: Used to validate strings. You can set a minimum or maximum length, enforce a regex pattern, or more.

  ```python
  from pydantic import constr

  class Animal(BaseModel):
      name: constr(min_length=3, max_length=50) # Must be 3-50 chars
      species: str
      age: conint(ge=0)
  ```

- `conint`: We've already seen this in action—it ensures that an integer falls within a specified range.

  ```python
  age: conint(ge=0, le=150)  # Age must be between 0 and 150
  ```

- **conlist**: Validates a list, allowing you to specify how many items can be in the list or even validate the type of items in the list.

-
    ```
    from pydantic import conlist

    class Zoo(BaseModel):
        animals: conlist(Animal, min_items=1)  # A zoo must have at least 1
    ```

---

2. Custom Validators

Pydantic also allows you to create custom validation methods within your models. For example, if you wanted to enforce that an animal's name cannot contain any numbers, you could write a custom validator like this:

```
from pydantic import BaseModel, validator

class Animal(BaseModel):
    name: str
    species: str
    age: conint(ge=0)

    @validator("name")
    def name_must_not_contain_numbers(cls, v):
        if any(char.isdigit() for char in v):
            raise ValueError("Name must not contain numbers")
        return v
```

Here, the custom validator checks the name field and raises an error if it contains any digits.

3. **Strict Types**

You can make data validation stricter by using **strict types** like `StrictInt` or `StrictStr`. These types enforce that the incoming data must be exactly of the specified type. For example:

```
from pydantic import StrictInt

class Animal(BaseModel):
    name: str
    species: str
    age: StrictInt   # Must be an integer, not a float or string
```

This enforces that the age must be an integer—no passing in strings like `"5"` or floats like `5.0`.

---

4. **Complex Nested Models**

Pydantic allows for the creation of **nested models**, where one model can be used as a field in another model. This is especially useful for validating complex JSON objects. For example:

```
class Animal(BaseModel):
    name: str
    species: str
    age: conint(ge=0)

class Zoo(BaseModel):
    name: str
    location: str
    animals: list[Animal]   # A list of Animal models
```

Here, the `Zoo` model contains a list of `Animal` models, and Pydantic will validate each animal in the list based on the rules defined in the `Animal` model.

5. Advanced Pydantic Features (Optional Fields, Aliases, and Default Values)

Pydantic offers more than just simple validation; it also provides advanced features like optional fields, aliases, and default values. Let's explore how these can add flexibility to your API's data models.

- **Optional fields**: Some fields may not always be present. You can define them as optional using Python's `Optional` type or `None` as the default value.

- **Field aliases**: When your API needs to interact with external systems, you may need to handle differently named fields. Pydantic's `alias` feature allows you to use alternate names for fields.

- **Default values**: You can set default values for fields, ensuring that your models behave consistently even when certain data is missing.

Here's how to implement all three:

```
from pydantic import BaseModel, Field
from typing import Optional

class Animal(BaseModel):
    name: str
    species: str
    age: int = Field(default=0, ge=0)  # Default age is 0, must be non-negative
    nickname: Optional[str] = None  # Optional field
    alias_name: str = Field(..., alias="full_name")  # alias for incoming data
```

This gives the API more flexibility, making it easy to handle optional, default, and aliased fields without breaking a sweat.

6. Common Validation Mistakes (and How to Avoid Them)

Even though Pydantic handles a lot of validation for you, there are still common mistakes developers might run into. Let's go over some of these pitfalls and how to avoid them:

- **Forgetting to Validate**: It's easy to forget validation in places where it's critical. For example, without Pydantic, you might assume certain fields are valid, only to run into issues later.

```python
# Mistake: Forgetting to validate age
def process_animal(animal: Animal):
    if animal.age < 0:
        print("Oops! Negative age!")
    else:
        print(f"{animal.name} the {animal.species} is {animal.age} years old.")

# Pydantic saves the day with automatic validation!
```

- **Assuming Data Will Always Be Clean**: Never assume that data coming into your API will be perfect. Users (and systems) make mistakes. Using Pydantic's automatic validation ensures you catch those mistakes early and avoid crashes.

- **Not Using the Right Types**: Make sure to use strict or constrained types (like `StrictInt`, `constr`, etc.) where necessary to avoid unexpected behavior.

By staying aware of these pitfalls, you can make sure your API always processes clean, validated data.

7. Creative Use Cases for Pydantic

Sometimes, Pydantic can be used in creative ways to add custom validation rules that make your API more robust (or just more fun!). Let's take a look at some examples:

- **Custom Validators**: You can define custom validation methods that enforce specific rules, such as making sure the name of an animal is "cool enough."

    ```python
    @validator("name")
    def check_coolness_of_name(cls, v):
        if v.lower() not in ["cool", "rad", "awesome"]:
            raise ValueError("The name is not cool enough!")
        return v
    ```

- **Validating External Data**: If your API needs to interact with external services, Pydantic models can be used to validate and transform incoming data, ensuring it's structured correctly before you process it.

- **Format Enforcement**: You can use custom validators to enforce specific formatting rules for fields like email addresses, URLs, or IDs.

Conclusion

In this chapter, we've separated our models into `model.py`, explored Pydantic's rich validation features, and dug into some advanced features like optional fields, aliases, and custom validators. With Pydantic, you're equipped to handle all sorts of data validation scenarios—whether it's basic constraints or more creative use cases.

Here's what our project folder structure looks like so far:

```
project/
├── main.py           # FastAPI app entry point
├── db.py             # Database connection logic
├── model.py          # Pydantic and SQLAlchemy models
├── tests/            # Directory for test files
│   └── test_main.py  # Your first unit test
├── .env              # Environment variables
└── requirements.txt  # List of dependencies
```

By keeping our code organized and flexible, we ensure that the API can handle any data thrown its way. In the next chapter, we'll dive into connecting our API to the database using **SQLAlchemy**, where we'll store and retrieve data.

Chapter 4: Storing and Retrieving Data – The SQLAlchemy Way

Now that we've set up our models and validation using Pydantic, it's time to store and retrieve data with **SQLAlchemy**. In this chapter, we'll explore SQLAlchemy's ORM (Object Relational Mapper), handle different database engines, and compare ORM to raw SQL queries for added flexibility.

Step 1: Install SQLAlchemy

Before we can dive into the database jungle, we need to install SQLAlchemy. Luckily, it's just one command away:

```
pip install sqlalchemy
```

With SQLAlchemy installed, we're ready to create our database connection. Think of SQLAlchemy as the translator between Python and your database—it speaks both languages fluently.

Step 2: Connect to a SQLite Database

For this example, we'll use **SQLite**—the pocketknife of databases. It's lightweight, server-less, and perfect for smaller projects or testing. Plus, it's already included with Python, so no extra installation is required!

In **db.py**, set up a connection to our SQLite database:

```python
from sqlalchemy import create_engine, Column, Integer, String
from sqlalchemy.ext.declarative import declarative_base
from sqlalchemy.orm import sessionmaker

DATABASE_URL = "sqlite:///./animals.db"

engine = create_engine(DATABASE_URL)
SessionLocal = sessionmaker(autocommit=False, autoflush=False, bind=engine)

Base = declarative_base()

class AnimalDB(Base):
    __tablename__ = "animals"

    id = Column(Integer, primary_key=True, index=True)
    name = Column(String, index=True)
    species = Column(String, index=True)
    age = Column(Integer)

Base.metadata.create_all(bind=engine)
```

This code does a few important things:

1. **Connects** to a SQLite database located at `./animals.db`. No need for complex setup—it's like having a pop-up campsite right in your backyard.
2. **Defines a table** called `animals` using a model class (`AnimalDB`), with columns for `id`, `name`, `species`, and `age`.
3. **Creates the table** if it doesn't already exist, making sure your animals have a place to live.

Step 3: Storing Animals in the Database

Now that we have a database set up, it's time to store some actual data—our animals! Instead of just returning a message, we'll store the animals in the database and give them IDs for easy tracking (like tagging animals in the wild, but more humane).

In `main.py`, update the `POST /animals/` endpoint to store the animal data in the database:

```python
from sqlalchemy.orm import Session
from fastapi import Depends
from .db import SessionLocal, AnimalDB

def get_db():
    db = SessionLocal()
    try:
        yield db
    finally:
        db.close()

@app.post("/animals/")
def create_animal(animal: Animal, db: Session = Depends(get_db)):
    animal_db = AnimalDB(name=animal.name, species=animal.species, age=animal.age)
    db.add(animal_db)
    db.commit()
    db.refresh(animal_db)
    return {"message": f"Added {animal.name} the {animal.species} to the database.", "id": animal_db.id}
```

Now, when someone adds an animal through your API, it'll be safely stored in the database. You'll also get back the newly created animal's ID, which makes it easier to track. It's like giving each animal a passport—now you know exactly where they are at all times!

Background on SQLAlchemy ORM

SQLAlchemy's **ORM** allows developers to interact with the database using Python objects rather than writing raw SQL queries. It simplifies complex queries and relationships, turning database tables into Python classes and rows into instances of those classes.

- **ORM Advantages**: With SQLAlchemy ORM, we can interact with the database in a more Pythonic way. For example, rather than writing a `SELECT` statement to retrieve an animal, we can simply query the **Animal** class and SQLAlchemy will take care of the rest.
- **Relationship Management**: The ORM makes it easy to manage relationships between tables (e.g., **Animal** and **Habitat**), allowing you to retrieve related data seamlessly.

SQLAlchemy also makes it easier to switch between different database engines, as we'll see when we cover MySQL and PostgreSQL.

A Comparison of ORM vs Raw SQL Queries

While **SQLAlchemy ORM** makes querying the database easier, there may be times when raw SQL queries are needed. Here's a quick comparison:

- **ORM Query**: This Pythonic approach abstracts SQL commands, making your code cleaner and more intuitive.

```
# ORM query: Get all animals
animals = db.query(Animal).all()
```

- **Raw SQL Query**: This gives you more control over the query but is less flexible if you switch databases.

```
# Raw SQL query: Get all animals
animals_raw = db.execute("SELECT * FROM animals")
```

While the ORM is typically easier to work with, raw SQL queries give you more control in certain situations, such as when running complex queries or needing database-specific optimizations.

Introducing Functional Tests with Pytest

In addition to unit testing, **functional testing** allows us to test the entire application to ensure that the routes, database, and business logic all work together as expected.

We'll use **pytest** for functional testing, making sure our database interactions and API endpoints are working correctly.

Let's set up a functional test to ensure animals can be successfully added and retrieved from the database:

```
from fastapi.testclient import TestClient
from .main import app
from .db import SessionLocal
import pytest

client = TestClient(app)

@pytest.fixture(scope="function")
def session():
    db = SessionLocal()
    yield db
    db.rollback()

def test_add_animal(session):
    response = client.post("/animals/", json={"name": "Larry", "species": "Leopard", "age": 5})
```

```
    assert response.status_code == 200
    # Check if the animal was added to the database
    animal =
session.query(Animal).filter_by(name="Larry").first()
    assert animal is not None
    assert animal.species == "Leopard"
```

This test checks that the API can add an animal to the database and that the animal data can be retrieved from the database.

Switching to MySQL or PostgreSQL

While **SQLite** is great for development, larger projects often require a more robust database like **MySQL** or **PostgreSQL**. Luckily, **SQLAlchemy** makes it easy to switch database engines with minimal changes to the code.

Switching to MySQL

To switch to **MySQL**, update the **SQLALCHEMY_DATABASE_URL** in db.py:

```
SQLALCHEMY_DATABASE_URL =
"mysql+pymysql://username:password@localhost/mydataba
se"
```

You'll also need to install the pymysql package to support MySQL:

```
pip install pymysql
```

With this small change, SQLAlchemy will now connect to a MySQL database instead of SQLite.

Switching to PostgreSQL

Similarly, to switch to **PostgreSQL**, update the **SQLALCHEMY_DATABASE_URL**:

```
SQLALCHEMY_DATABASE_URL =
"postgresql://username:password@localhost/mydatabase"
```

And install the `psycopg2` package:

```
pip install psycopg2
```

Just like with MySQL, SQLAlchemy will now connect to a PostgreSQL database with minimal changes to the codebase.

One of the greatest strengths of SQLAlchemy is its flexibility. With the same models and query logic, you can easily switch between different database engines depending on the needs of your project. By centralizing the database connection logic in `db.py`, you can keep the rest of your application unchanged, ensuring that the switch between development (SQLite) and production (MySQL/PostgreSQL) is seamless.

Conclusion

In this chapter, we've explored SQLAlchemy ORM and how it simplifies interactions with the database, compared ORM with raw SQL queries, and set up functional testing using **pytest**. These tools and techniques will ensure that your API is robust, flexible, and ready for real-world use.

Chapter 5: Bringing It All Together – Building a Full-Stack Front-End with Jinja2

Congratulations! You've built the core of your API and now we're ready to complete the full-stack experience by adding a dynamic front-end using **Jinja2**. This chapter will walk you through creating templates that pull data from your database and display it on a front-end page. We'll start by creating a base template, building an index page, and finish with an upsert form to insert and update animals. Once we're done, you'll have a fully functioning full-stack application—database, back-end, and front-end, all working in harmony.

Step 1: Setting Up Jinja2 Templates

Jinja2 is FastAPI's go-to tool for rendering dynamic HTML pages. This allows us to build templates that pull data from the back-end and render it as beautiful, functional HTML.

First, we need to set up the directory structure for the templates. Create a `templates/` folder in the root of your project:

```
project/
├── main.py
├── db.py
├── model.py
├── templates/
│   ├── base.html
│   └── index.html
├── tests/
└── requirements.txt
```

Our templates will live inside the `templates/` directory, and we'll start by creating a reusable **base template**. This template will contain common layout elements like headers, footers, and a main content block that can be overridden by specific pages.

Here's what **base.html** might look like:

```html
<!DOCTYPE html>
<html lang="en">
<head>
    <meta charset="UTF-8">
    <meta name="viewport" content="width=device-width, initial-scale=1.0">
    <title>{{ title }}</title>
</head>
<body>
    <header>
        <h1>Welcome to the API Jungle! 🐾</h1>
    </header>
    <main>
        {% block content %}{% endblock %}
    </main>
    <footer>
        <p>&copy; 2024 The API Jungle</p>
    </footer>
</body>
</html>
```

This base template sets up the core structure of every page, so we don't need to repeat this HTML in every individual template. Instead, we'll use **block content** to insert page-specific information like lists or forms.

Step 2: Creating the Index Page

The next step is to create the index page, which will extend the **base.html** template and display a list of animals from the database. In FastAPI, we'll use Jinja2 to pull in the data and render it dynamically.

Here's the directory structure after adding **index.html**:

```
project/
├── main.py
├── db.py
├── model.py
├── templates/
│   ├── base.html
│   └── index.html
├── tests/
└── requirements.txt
```

In **index.html**, we'll extend the base template and insert a list of animals into the content block:

```
{% extends "base.html" %}
{% block content %}
    <h2>{{ title }}</h2>
    <ul>
        {% for animal in animals %}
            <li>{{ animal.name }} the {{ animal.species }} (Age: {{ animal.age }})</li>
        {% endfor %}
    </ul>
{% endblock %}
```

This page will display a list of animals from the database. FastAPI will pull the data in, and Jinja2 will handle rendering it as HTML.

Step 3: Setting Up the Route to Render the Page

Now that our templates are ready, let's hook them up to the backend by creating a route that serves the index page and passes the animal data to it. We'll do this in `main.py` by adding a route for the home page (/).

Update **main.py** to include the following:

```python
from fastapi import FastAPI, Depends
from fastapi.templating import Jinja2Templates
from sqlalchemy.orm import Session
from fastapi import Request
from .db import SessionLocal, AnimalDB

app = FastAPI()
templates = Jinja2Templates(directory="templates")

def get_db():
    db = SessionLocal()
    try:
        yield db
    finally:
        db.close()

@app.get("/")
def index(request: Request, db: Session = Depends(get_db)):
    animals = db.query(AnimalDB).all()
    return templates.TemplateResponse("index.html", {"request": request, "title": "Our Jungle Residents", "animals": animals})
```

This route does several important things:

- **Queries the database** for all animals using SQLAlchemy.
- **Passes the data** (the list of animals) to the **index.html** template.
- Renders the template dynamically using Jinja2.

Now, when users visit the home page (/), they'll see a dynamic list of animals pulled directly from the database.

Step 4: Testing the Route

Testing is an important part of the development cycle, especially when adding new features. Let's add a simple functional test to ensure our index route is working correctly.

Here's how the project structure looks now, including the test file:

```
project/
├── main.py
├── db.py
├── model.py
├── templates/
│   ├── base.html
│   └── index.html
├── tests/
│   └── test_main.py
└── requirements.txt
```

In **test_main.py**, add a test for the index route:

```python
from fastapi.testclient import TestClient
from .main import app

client = TestClient(app)

def test_index():
    response = client.get("/")
    assert response.status_code == 200
    assert b"Welcome to the API Jungle!" in response.content
```

This test will check whether the index page loads successfully and includes the welcome message from the **base.html** template.

Step 5: Congratulations! You're Full-Stack Now!

That's it! You've officially built a full-stack application. You've got a FastAPI back-end, a Jinja2 front-end, and a database powering it all. Give yourself a pat on the back—you're now a full-stack developer.

But wait, there's more! In the next step, we'll create an **upsert form** that will allow you to add and update animals directly from the front-end.

Step 6: Building the Upsert Form

The next feature we'll add is an **upsert form** that lets users insert or update animals in the database. This form will allow us to either add new animals or edit existing ones. We'll create a new **upsert.html** template for this.

The directory structure now looks like this:

```
project/
├── main.py
├── db.py
├── model.py
├── templates/
│   ├── base.html
│   ├── index.html
│   └── upsert.html
├── tests/
│   └── test_main.py
└── requirements.txt
```

In **upsert.html**, create a form for adding or editing animals:

```
{% extends "base.html" %}

{% block content %}
    <h2>{{ title }}</h2>
    <form method="post" action="/upsert/">
        <label for="name">Animal Name:</label>
        <input type="text" id="name" name="name" value="{{ animal.name if animal else '' }}">
        <br>
        <label for="species">Species:</label>
        <input type="text" id="species" name="species" value="{{ animal.species if animal else '' }}">
        <br>
        <label for="age">Age:</label>
        <input type="number" id="age" name="age" value="{{ animal.age if animal else '' }}">
```

```
            <br>
            <button type="submit">Save Animal</button>
        </form>
{% endblock %}
```

This form checks whether we're adding a new animal or editing an existing one based on whether `animal` is passed into the template.

Step 7: Handling Form Submissions

In **main.py**, we'll create a route to handle form submissions, allowing users to insert new animals or update existing ones:

```
from fastapi import Form

@app.post("/upsert/")
def upsert_animal(name: str = Form(...), species: str = Form(...), age: int = Form(...), db: Session = Depends(get_db)):
    animal = db.query(AnimalDB).filter_by(name=name).first()
    if animal:
        # Update existing animal
        animal.species = species
        animal.age = age
    else:
        # Insert new animal
        animal = AnimalDB(name=name, species=species, age=age)
        db.add(animal)
    db.commit()
    return {"message": f"Saved {animal.name} the {animal.species} (Age: {animal.age}) to the database."}
```

This route checks if the animal already exists in the database and either updates the record or inserts a new one. With this, users can now manage animals directly from the front-end!

With this setup, you've now built a full-stack web application that handles both data retrieval and user input. You're truly full-stack!

Chapter 6: CRUD – The Backbone of Every API (and Our Jungle)

APIs, much like jungle safaris, thrive on **CRUD** operations—**Create, Read, Update, Delete**. Whether you're adding a new animal to the jungle (Create), observing them from afar (Read), updating their records (Update), or sometimes saying goodbye (Delete), CRUD is the essence of managing any application's data.

In this chapter, we'll take a safari through CRUD, exploring how it works in our jungle-themed API. By the end, you'll be an expert at managing the creatures in your digital jungle. We'll also discuss the broader system architecture—think of it as mapping out the wildlife reserves of your API ecosystem.

1. What is CRUD?

In the wild world of API development, CRUD operations form the basic actions for managing data:

- **Create**: Like introducing a new species to the jungle, **Create** adds fresh data to the system.
- **Read**: Think of it as observing animals in the wild. You're retrieving data without making any changes.
- **Update**: Sometimes, animals age or change habitats. The **Update** operation lets you modify existing records.
- **Delete**: Although rare, some animals leave the jungle. **Delete** removes data when it's no longer needed.

Together, these operations allow you to manage the digital creatures of your API jungle.

2. CRUD in Our API

Let's swing from vine to vine through the trees as we review how CRUD works in our API. We've been steadily building out each of these operations, but let's ensure we're covering every part of the jungle.

Create: Adding New Animals

We've already tackled **Create** by adding new animals to the database. Much like welcoming new animals to the jungle, this operation ensures that our database continues to grow.

Here's how we've implemented **Create** in the **upsert form**:

```
@app.post("/upsert/")
def upsert_animal(name: str = Form(...), species: str = Form(...), age: int = Form(...), db: Session = Depends(get_db)):
    animal = AnimalDB(name=name, species=species, age=age)
    db.add(animal)
    db.commit()
    return {"message": f"Added {animal.name} to the database."}
```

This route allows users to add new animals to the database. It's like expanding the jungle with new and exciting species!

Read: Observing Animals

Observing animals in the wild is the **Read** operation of our API. We pull data from the database and display it, much like documenting the various species roaming the jungle.

Here's how we've implemented **Read** in the **index** route:

```
@app.get("/")
def index(request: Request, db: Session = Depends(get_db)):
    animals = db.query(AnimalDB).all()
    return templates.TemplateResponse("index.html", {"request": request, "animals": animals})
```

In this route, we query the database for all animals and render them dynamically in the front-end. It's the digital version of a safari tour, allowing users to observe animals in their natural (or database) habitat.

Update: Keeping Track of Changes

Just like in the jungle, sometimes our data needs updating. Animals age, change species (not scientifically accurate but fun for an API), or even move habitats. The **Update** operation allows us to modify existing records.

Here's how we've implemented **Update**:

```
@app.put("/animals/{animal_id}")
def update_animal(animal_id: int, animal: Animal, db: Session = Depends(get_db)):
    animal_db = db.query(AnimalDB).filter(AnimalDB.id == animal_id).first()
    if not animal_db:
        raise HTTPException(status_code=404, detail="Animal not found")

    animal_db.name = animal.name
    animal_db.species = animal.species
    animal_db.age = animal.age
    db.commit()
    return {"message": f"Updated {animal.name} in the database."}
```

This endpoint allows users to update records in the database—keeping the jungle records accurate and up to date.

Delete: Saying Goodbye

Every now and then, an animal leaves the jungle, and we need to remove them from the system. **Delete** lets us clean up our database and keep the data ecosystem healthy.

Here's how we handle **Delete** in our API:

```
@app.delete("/animals/{animal_id}")
def delete_animal(animal_id: int, db: Session = Depends(get_db)):
    animal_db = db.query(AnimalDB).filter(AnimalDB.id == animal_id).first()
    if not animal_db:
        raise HTTPException(status_code=404, detail="Animal not found")

    db.delete(animal_db)
    db.commit()
    return {"message": f"Deleted animal with id {animal_id} from the database."}
```

With this endpoint, users can remove animals from the database when they're no longer needed.

3. System Architecture in Our API Jungle

Now that we've completed the CRUD cycle, let's zoom out and look at the bigger picture. In any well-managed jungle, each animal plays its role—and in an API, each layer contributes to the system's overall health.

Here's how the architecture of our API jungle looks:

- **Database Layer (SQLAlchemy)**: This is the ground where our data lives and breathes. SQLAlchemy's ORM acts as the bridge between our Python code and the database, translating complex SQL queries into Pythonic objects.

- **Back-End Layer (FastAPI)**: FastAPI is the jungle guide that manages incoming requests, fetches data from the database, and returns responses. Each CRUD operation corresponds to a route, allowing users to interact with the data.

- **Front-End Layer (Jinja2)**: The animals need a place to be displayed, and that's where the front-end comes in. By rendering **Jinja2** templates, we create a dynamic front-end that pulls data from the back-end and presents it in an easily digestible format.

- **Security Measures (JWT)**: In our jungle, we need to keep the predators (hackers) out. By implementing **JWT authentication**, we ensure that only authorized users can interact with the data.

Conclusion: Navigating the Jungle

CRUD operations are the backbone of every API, just like the food chain in a real jungle. Each operation—**Create, Read, Update, and Delete**—plays an essential role in managing and maintaining data. By understanding these operations, and how they fit into the larger system architecture, you're now fully equipped to navigate your API jungle with confidence.

Chapter 7: Securing Your API – Fortifying Your Jungle Camp

APIs, while powerful, are vulnerable to a variety of attacks if not properly secured. In this chapter, we'll start with an implementation of the **FastAPI Simple Security** option, which is suitable for smaller applications or development environments. Then, we'll transition to a more robust and scalable security model using **JWT (JSON Web Tokens)** for production-level deployments.

We'll guide you step by step, including environment variable management to secure sensitive information, and ensure that by the end of this chapter, your API is fortified and ready for the wild jungle of the internet.

---

1. Implementing FastAPI Simple Security

For smaller applications or early stages of development, **FastAPI Simple Security** provides an easy-to-use API key-based authentication system. It's perfect for securing access to your API without much overhead.

Step 1: Installing Simple Security

First, install the **fastapi-simple-security** package:

```
pip install fastapi-simple-security
```

Step 2: Configuring Simple Security

In your **main.py** file, you'll need to import and configure **FastAPI Simple Security**:

```python
from fastapi_simple_security import api_key_router, api_key_security

app = FastAPI()

app.include_router(api_key_router, prefix="/auth", tags=["auth"])
```

This configuration includes a new authentication route under **/auth/** that handles creating and managing API keys.

Step 3: Protecting Routes with API Keys

Now, we'll secure a route using **api_key_security**:

```python
@app.get("/secure-data/",
dependencies=[Depends(api_key_security)])
def read_secure_data():
    return {"message": "This is protected data!"}
```

Any request to **/secure-data/** now requires a valid API key to access.

2. Securing Secrets with Environment Variables

Hard-coding API keys and secrets in your code can expose sensitive information. To mitigate this risk, we'll store them in an **.env** file and load them securely into the application.

Here's an example of what your **.env** file might look like:

```
FASTAPI_SIMPLE_SECURITY_DB_LOCATION="./sqlite2.db"
FASTAPI_SIMPLE_SECURITY_SECRET="justletmein"
FAST_API_SIMPLE_SECURITY_AUTOMATIC_EXPIRATION="3"
```

To load these environment variables in FastAPI, we'll use **python-dotenv**:

```
pip install python-dotenv
```

In your **main.py**, load the environment variables like this:

```
from dotenv import load_dotenv
import os

load_dotenv()

SECRET_KEY = os.getenv("FASTAPI_SIMPLE_SECURITY_SECRET")
```

Now your sensitive keys and secrets are securely stored in the **.env** file and accessed via environment variables.

---

3. Transitioning to JWT Authentication

While **FastAPI Simple Security** is great for small-scale apps, **JWT** provides a stronger, more flexible way to manage authentication for production environments. Let's walk through the transition from API keys to **JWT authentication**, where we generate tokens, secure routes, and manage token expiration.

1. Why Migrate from API Keys to JWT?

FastAPI Simple Security provides a basic API key mechanism that works well for single-server or small-scale applications. However, in production-grade environments, **JWT (JSON Web Tokens)** offers a more secure, scalable, and flexible authentication system.

- **Short-lived tokens**: JWT tokens come with expiration times, which limit their validity if compromised.
- **Stateless**: Unlike API keys, which might require server-side management, JWT tokens are stateless and can be verified using a secret or public/private key.

- **More control**: With JWT, you can control permissions, scopes, and roles, adding flexibility for complex applications.

2. Implementation Overview

Let's walk through the necessary steps for migrating from **API keys** to **JWT authentication**, ensuring each step is clear for the end user. We'll include code snippets, configuration, and testing examples to guide users through securing their application with JWT.

3. JWT Configuration

Step 1: Generating JWT Tokens

We'll begin by generating JWT tokens during the login process. These tokens will be passed back to the user and included in future requests to authenticate them.

```python
from datetime import datetime, timedelta
from jose import JWTError, jwt

SECRET_KEY = "mysecretkey"  # Use environment variables in production
ALGORITHM = "HS256"
ACCESS_TOKEN_EXPIRE_MINUTES = 30  # Tokens expire after 30 minutes

def create_access_token(data: dict):
    to_encode = data.copy()
    expire = datetime.utcnow() + timedelta(minutes=ACCESS_TOKEN_EXPIRE_MINUTES)
    to_encode.update({"exp": expire})
    encoded_jwt = jwt.encode(to_encode, SECRET_KEY, algorithm=ALGORITHM)
    return encoded_jwt
```

Here, we define a function that generates a JWT with an expiration time, using **HS256** for encryption. The token will include user information and an expiration timestamp.

Step 2: User Login and Token Generation

The next step is to create a login endpoint that authenticates users and returns a JWT token.

```python
from fastapi import Depends, HTTPException, status
from pydantic import BaseModel

class Token(BaseModel):
    access_token: str
    token_type: str

@app.post("/token/", response_model=Token)
def login_for_access_token(username: str, password: str):
    if username != "admin" or password != "password":
        raise HTTPException(status_code=status.HTTP_401_UNAUTHORIZED, detail="Incorrect username or password")

    access_token = create_access_token(data={"sub": username})
    return {"access_token": access_token, "token_type": "bearer"}
```

In this **/token/** endpoint:

- The server authenticates the user.
- Upon successful login, it generates a JWT token and returns it to the client.

4. Securing API Endpoints with JWT

Now that we've created tokens, the next step is securing our routes. We'll need to validate incoming JWT tokens with each request to ensure that only authorized users can access protected routes.

```python
from fastapi import Depends, HTTPException
from fastapi.security import OAuth2PasswordBearer

oauth2_scheme = OAuth2PasswordBearer(tokenUrl="token")

def verify_token(token: str = Depends(oauth2_scheme)):
    credentials_exception = HTTPException(status_code=status.HTTP_401_UNAUTHORIZED, detail="Invalid authentication credentials")
    try:
        payload = jwt.decode(token, SECRET_KEY, algorithms=[ALGORITHM])
        username: str = payload.get("sub")
        if username is None:
            raise credentials_exception
    except JWTError:
        raise credentials_exception
    return username

@app.get("/secure-route/")
def secure_route(user: str = Depends(verify_token)):
    return {"message": f"Hello, {user}! Welcome to the secure route."}
```

This **/secure-route/** endpoint is now protected by JWT authentication. If a valid token is provided in the **Authorization** header, the request is granted access.

5. Transitioning from API Keys to JWT: The Migration Guide

This section will guide users through the steps required to transition from the simpler **FastAPI Simple Security** (API key-based) to the more robust **JWT implementation**:

- **Step 1: Update Configuration** – Replace API key dependencies with JWT verification functions.
- **Step 2: Create JWT tokens** – Introduce token generation on login.
- **Step 3: Secure Endpoints** – Replace API key checks with JWT validation for protected routes.
- **Step 4: Implement Token Expiration** – Add token expiration to increase security by limiting the token's lifespan.

For a smooth migration, we'll include code for both authentication and validation, providing a step-by-step walkthrough for updating the app without disrupting existing functionality.

---

6. Testing JWT Security

Just as important as the implementation is testing to ensure that the security mechanisms work as expected. We'll provide functional tests that validate the security measures in place.

```python
from fastapi.testclient import TestClient
from .main import app

client = TestClient(app)

def test_login():
    response = client.post("/token/",
data={"username": "admin", "password": "password"})
    assert response.status_code == 200
    assert "access_token" in response.json()

def test_secure_route():
    login_response = client.post("/token/",
data={"username": "admin", "password": "password"})
    token = login_response.json()["access_token"]

    headers = {"Authorization": f"Bearer {token}"}
    response = client.get("/secure-route/",
headers=headers)
    assert response.status_code == 200
    assert "Hello, admin!" in response.json()
["message"]
```

These tests will ensure that:

1. **Login** functionality returns a valid JWT token.
2. Protected routes are only accessible with a valid JWT token.

---

7. Final Thoughts on JWT Security

By transitioning from API key-based security to JWT, you're adopting a more robust and scalable approach to authentication. JWT allows for token expiration, is stateless, and integrates well with role-based access control (RBAC) and other advanced security mechanisms.

Security Starts at Day One: The Developer's Responsibility

We've all been there—knee-deep in code, trying to hit deadlines, and adding **"we'll fix it later"** to the list of things to address. But when it comes to security, "later" can quickly turn into "too late." Cybersecurity isn't just the concern of operations teams or network administrators; it's a fundamental part of development, and the sooner it's baked into the code, the safer the application will be.

The truth is, **every developer is the first line of defense** in building secure applications. Hackers don't wait for your app to hit production before they start looking for cracks in the armor. Vulnerabilities introduced in the development phase—whether due to poor input validation, weak authentication, or just plain old neglect—are the seeds of tomorrow's breaches. And here's the kicker: once your app is compromised, it's not just the company that loses. It's the developers too. Data breaches cost time, trust, and professional credibility.

Preventing a Breach Before It Starts

Here's a fun fact (if you like the kind of fun that keeps you up at night): the vast majority of breaches are the result of **preventable vulnerabilities**. You don't need to be a cybersecurity expert to secure your app; you just need to follow best practices and stay vigilant. Think of security as hygiene—simple, daily habits that, when followed, dramatically reduce the risk of infection (or in this case, intrusion).

At the development level, it means:

- **Sanitizing inputs** like you're prepping for surgery.

- **Validating data** with the same care you'd check a bridge before crossing.
- And, of course, **encrypting sensitive data** like it's your Netflix password.

Small, consistent efforts prevent major catastrophes. If you take care of security from day one, you're not just creating functional code—you're building trust.

Security Is Not Sexy, But It Should Be

Now, I get it—security doesn't exactly scream "exciting." You're more likely to talk about new frameworks or exciting features than input validation and token expiration. But here's the thing: **security should be sexy.** Think about it: what's cooler than building something that works *and* stands up to a hacker's worst efforts? What's more impressive than an app that handles everything thrown at it while keeping its data locked down tight?

At the end of the day, developers who prioritize security are developers who care about the future—not just of their app, but of their users. And that's something to be proud of.

Evangelizing Security to the Next Generation of Developers

I've spent a career in IT, and if there's one thing I've learned, it's that cybersecurity isn't something you "graduate" to later. It's a mindset that starts from the first line of code. We need to evangelize security at every level of development—not as an afterthought but as an integral part of the process. This is about ensuring that the next generation of developers understands that their role goes beyond features and deadlines; it extends to protecting users and safeguarding data.

So, yes, I'll keep beating this drum. Because while security may not be the flashiest part of development, it's undoubtedly one of the most important.

Chapter 8: Mastering FastAPI's /docs – Your Built-In Testing Ground

FastAPI comes packed with tools to make your life as a developer easier, and one of its most powerful, yet often underutilized features is the built-in **Swagger UI** available at `/docs`. This isn't just documentation—it's an **interactive testing ground** for your API.

While many frameworks leave you to fend for yourself when it comes to documenting and testing APIs, FastAPI steps up and says, **"I got this!"** In this chapter, we'll explore how FastAPI's automatic documentation can save you hours of time and frustration by allowing you to test your API directly from the browser. No need for Postman, curl, or any third-party tools—everything you need is right here.

---

1. Accessing Swagger UI, OpenAPI, and ReDoc

FastAPI automatically generates three types of documentation that can be accessed directly in your browser:

- **Swagger UI**: The default interactive documentation at `/docs`. This provides a fully interactive interface where you can test all API routes.

  How to access: Go to `http://127.0.0.1:8000/docs` in your browser to see the list of API routes.

- **OpenAPI Schema**: FastAPI generates an OpenAPI schema, which provides a machine-readable representation of your API's structure and routes.

How to access: Visit `http://127.0.0.1:8000/openapi.json` to view the OpenAPI JSON schema.

- **ReDoc**: An alternative to Swagger UI, ReDoc provides a cleaner, read-only interface for viewing your API's documentation.

  How to access: Go to `http://127.0.0.1:8000/redoc` to view your API's documentation using ReDoc.

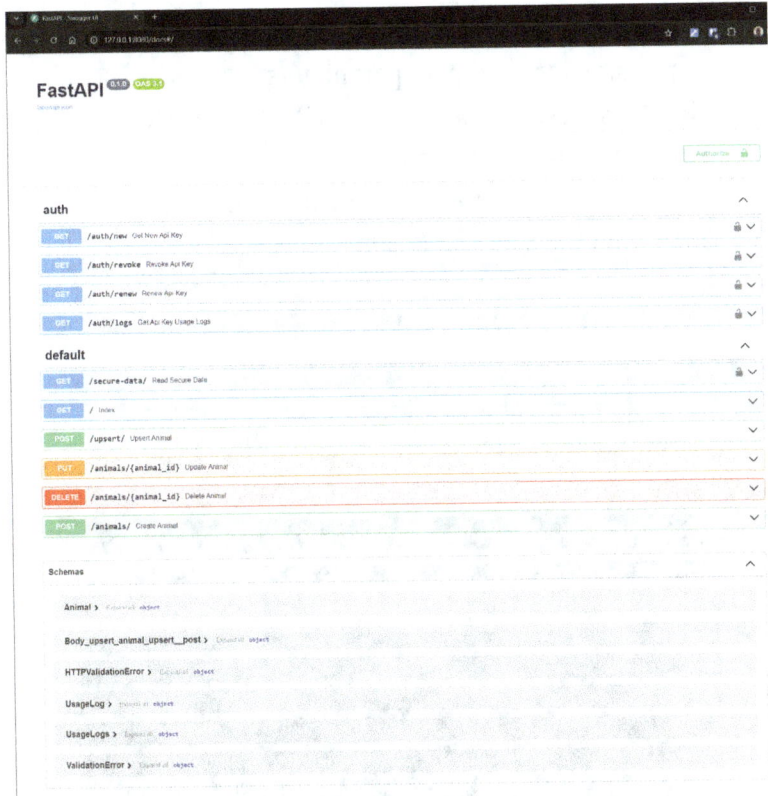

2. Testing Endpoints with Swagger UI

The real magic of **/docs** is the ability to test your endpoints directly. By clicking on any route in the Swagger UI, you can send requests, pass parameters, and inspect the API's response all in one place. Think of it like **Postman** but without the extra setup.

Let's say you have an endpoint to retrieve animal data. By navigating to `/docs`, you'll see a list of your API's routes, and you can click on the one you want to test. From there, Swagger UI lets you:

- **Input parameters**: You can test different query parameters or send path parameters.
- **Send requests**: Whether it's a **GET** or **POST** request, you can trigger it directly from the UI.
- **Check the responses**: Review the API's response, including the status code and body.

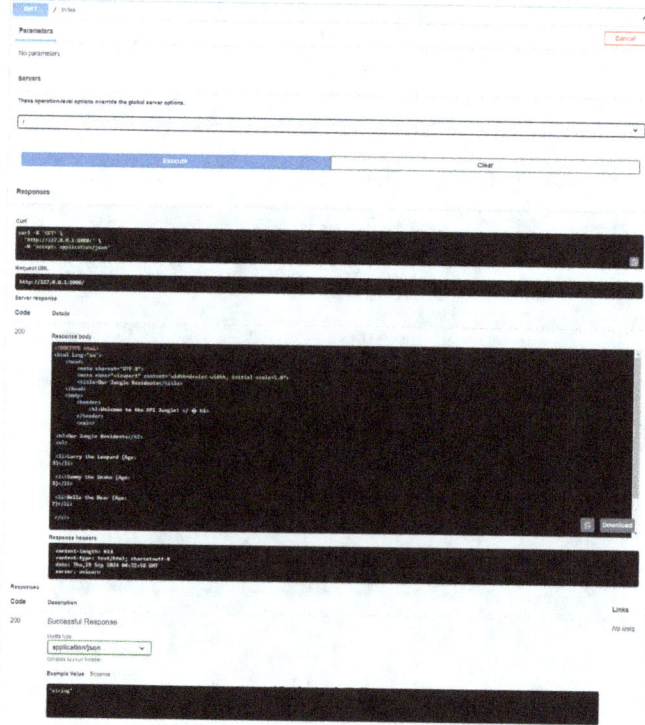

3. Authenticating in Swagger UI Using JWT

To secure some of your routes using JWT, Swagger UI also allows you to authenticate by providing a **Bearer token**. Here's how you can authenticate your requests in Swagger:

Step 1: Generate a JWT token

First, use your API's `/token/` endpoint to log in and retrieve a JWT token:

```
curl -X 'POST' \
  'http://127.0.0.1:8000/token/' \
  -H 'Content-Type: application/x-www-form-urlencoded' \
  -d 'username=admin&password=password'
```

This will return a token in the format:

```
{
  "access_token": "your_jwt_token",
  "token_type": "bearer"
}
```

Step 2: Authenticate in Swagger UI

1. Navigate to the **Authorize** button in the top-right corner of the Swagger UI page.

2. Enter your **Bearer token** (the JWT token generated from the `/token/` endpoint) in the following format:

   ```
   Bearer your_jwt_token
   ```

3. Click **Authorize**. Swagger will now automatically include the token in the headers for any requests to protected endpoints.

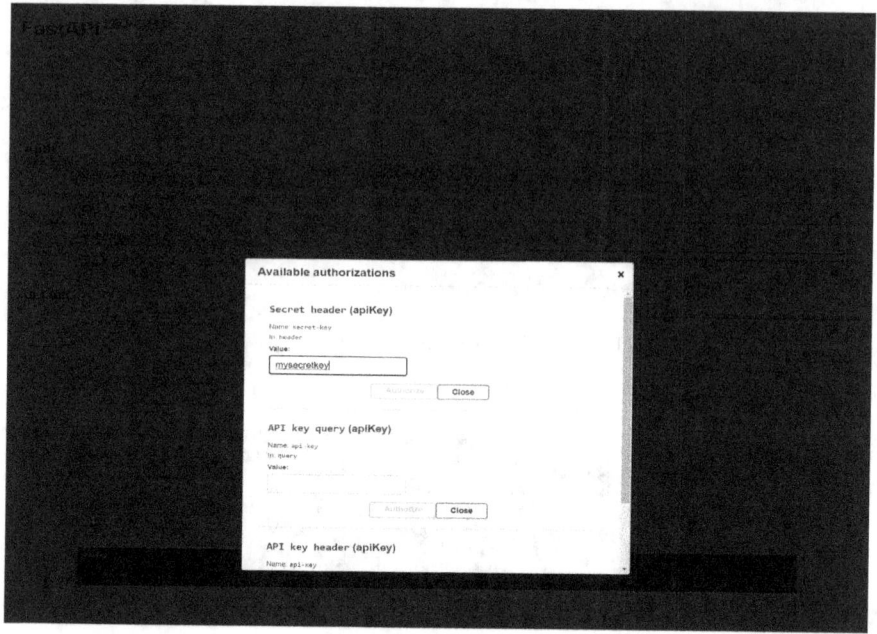

4. The Benefits of Using /docs

Why should you use /docs? Beyond the obvious time savings, here are some key benefits of Swagger UI:

- **Interactive Testing**: Unlike traditional docs, Swagger lets you test your API right from the browser, helping you debug issues faster.
- **Always In Sync**: Since FastAPI generates the docs based on your code, you never have to worry about documentation becoming outdated. The docs evolve as your API does.
- **Perfect for Collaboration**: You can share the /docs link with teammates, QA testers, or even business stakeholders who need to explore the API without needing to install third-party tools.

According to an Udemy blog post, many developers cite this feature as a key reason why they prefer FastAPI over alternatives like Flask or Django. Having live, interactive documentation baked into the framework cuts down on the need for external tools.

5. Customizing Your /docs

FastAPI's built-in documentation doesn't just stop at auto-generation—you can fully customize it. Whether you want to change the title, description, or hide sensitive routes, FastAPI gives you full control over what's visible.

Here's how you can customize your Swagger UI:

```python
app = FastAPI(title="My Awesome API",
description="API for managing jungle animals.")
```

You can also hide routes, such as an admin-only route, from appearing in the docs:

```python
from fastapi.openapi.utils import get_openapi

def custom_openapi():
    if app.openapi_schema:
        return app.openapi_schema
    openapi_schema = get_openapi(
        title="Custom API",
        version="1.0.0",
        description="This API manages the jungle.",
        routes=[route for route in app.routes if route.path != "/admin"]
    )
    app.openapi_schema = openapi_schema
    return openapi_schema

app.openapi = custom_openapi
```

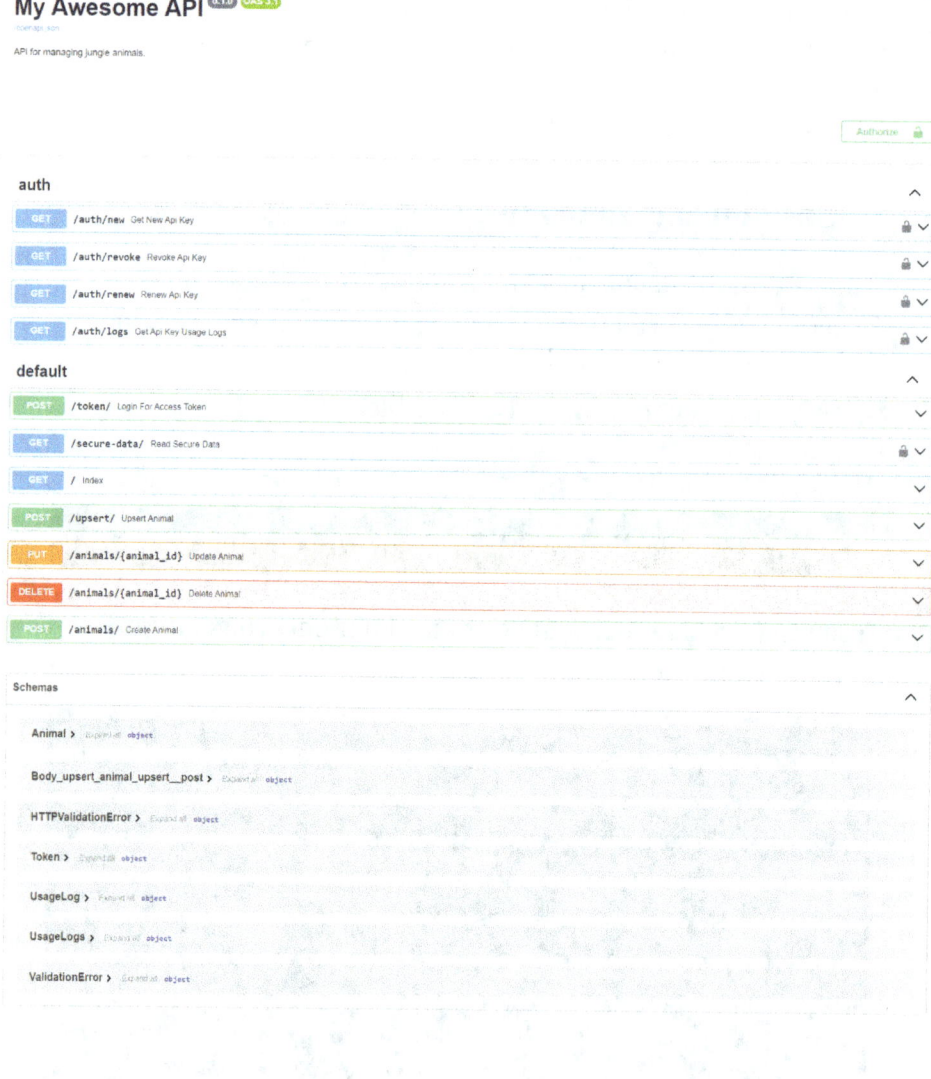

6. Advanced Features and Hidden Power

In addition to testing basic requests, Swagger UI offers several advanced features:

- **POST Requests**: Test POST routes by sending complex JSON payloads directly from the browser.
- **JWT Tokens**: Authenticate users using JWTs, sending tokens in headers for protected routes.
- **Schema Validation**: Automatically validates request and response schemas based on your Pydantic models.

Conclusion: Swagger UI – The Automatic Documentation You Didn't Know You Needed

API documentation often gets treated like the dishes—you know you have to do it, but you'll gladly put it off if you can. Enter **Swagger**: the magical dishwashing machine that does it for you. Every endpoint you create in FastAPI is automatically documented, complete with request parameters, expected responses, and even error codes.

No more painstaking manual updates to your API documentation every time you tweak an endpoint. Swagger's docs update themselves as you add or modify routes in your code, keeping everything current without any extra effort from you. It's like discovering you had an extra hour in the day—time you can now spend building features instead of documenting them.

Real-World Time Saver: Say Goodbye to Testing Headaches

Swagger's real value shines when it comes to testing. Traditional API testing usually involves tools like **Postman** or **cURL**, where you manually write out the HTTP requests, attach payloads, and try to remember how everything fits together. With Swagger, the API itself becomes the testing tool.

Here's a scenario where Swagger feels like the best thing since sliced bread:

- You've just added a new endpoint to your API, let's say `POST /animals/`.
- Without Swagger, you'd open Postman or another tool, manually type in the URL, add your headers, format the JSON body, and hope you got everything right.
- But with Swagger, you just open your browser, go to `http://127.0.0.1:8000/docs`, find the endpoint, fill in the data fields, and hit **Try it out**.

Swagger does all the heavy lifting for you, formatting the request, sending it to your API, and even showing you the response. It's like ordering takeout instead of cooking—except this meal is always prepared perfectly.

Simplifying Teamwork and Collaboration

When you're working solo, documentation is more of a personal reminder. But the moment you collaborate with a team—or open your API to the public—documentation becomes critical. Swagger's **OpenAPI integration** turns your API into a living, breathing manual that anyone can interact with.

Picture this: You're working with a team of developers across different time zones. Communication can be tricky, and explaining each endpoint's nuances can take more time than actually coding them. But with Swagger, your API's documentation is always up-to-date, and anyone on the team can immediately understand how to interact with it. Front-end developers can explore the API, testers can run checks right from their browsers, and new team members can jump in without hunting down outdated docs.

Swagger makes team collaboration a breeze:

1. **Exploration Made Easy**: Developers can test API routes without opening another app—they can just try it out directly from the docs page.
2. **Quick Debugging**: Imagine adding a new route, and something goes wrong. Instead of spinning up Postman, you can try the endpoint in Swagger, providing an instant playground to check the request-response cycle.
3. **Seamless Integration**: Because OpenAPI is the gold standard for API documentation, Swagger docs can be exported and shared with external developers or third-party services.

Better Error Handling and Debugging – It's All Right There

Errors happen. APIs break, and things don't always work as expected. This is where Swagger really shines. Instead of hunting through logs or scouring error messages, Swagger shows you exactly where things go wrong.

When you test an endpoint that's misbehaving, Swagger gives you a full breakdown of the error:

- **Status Codes**: See exactly what status code the API returned, be it a 404, 500, or something else.
- **Error Messages**: Proper error handling in FastAPI means that Swagger will show you the error message right in the UI.
- **Response Details**: See the exact response body, so you know what went wrong at a glance.

Because Swagger docs are interactive, you can tweak the request and try again instantly, speeding up the debugging process. No more blindly firing requests into the void—it's like having night vision goggles in the jungle: suddenly, everything becomes crystal clear.

Automated Client Generation: Build Once, Deploy Everywhere

One of Swagger's lesser-known but incredibly powerful features is its ability to generate client code automatically. Suppose you've built an API and need a front-end to interact with it. Instead of manually writing client-side code, Swagger's OpenAPI schema can generate the client for you.

Tools that work with OpenAPI can generate client libraries in various programming languages, like:

- A **JavaScript** client for web apps.
- A **Python** client for machine learning scripts.
- A **TypeScript** client for **React** applications.

This "set it and forget it" feature saves countless hours in multi-platform development. With Swagger, your API becomes a universal tool—accessible from anywhere, by anything. It's like building a Swiss Army knife with a blade for every programming language.

Swagger + Testing Frameworks = Smooth Integration

If you're a fan of automated testing (and who isn't?), Swagger's integration with OpenAPI can speed up your test-writing process. By using tools like **pytest** alongside OpenAPI-generated schemas, you can automate testing with minimal effort.

Imagine having your API automatically tested for:

- **Response Validation**: Ensuring the API returns the correct data structure.
- **Status Codes**: Verifying the right status codes are returned for different conditions.
- **Security Checks**: Making sure secured endpoints behave as expected.

Swagger helps validate your API's behavior and can work seamlessly with testing frameworks, ensuring your API runs smoothly.

Extolling the Swagger/Testing Connection: A Developer's Dream

In typical development, testing is where APIs can trip up. But using FastAPI with Swagger and OpenAPI makes the testing process straightforward:

1. **Quick Scenario Testing**: Change parameters directly in Swagger and rerun tests without rewriting test cases.

2. **Demonstration Tool**: Swagger's UI makes it incredibly easy to show off your API to non-technical stakeholders.
3. **Documenting Edge Cases**: Swagger helps test for unusual inputs and document the behavior for unexpected conditions.

In short, FastAPI + Swagger isn't just about documentation—it's an all-in-one toolkit for building, testing, and deploying high-quality APIs.

Chapter 9: Performance Tuning and Scalability – Taming the API Jungle

Building a robust API isn't just about getting the endpoints right; it's about ensuring that your API performs efficiently and scales seamlessly as demand grows. Whether you're dealing with hundreds of users in a proof-of-concept (POC) or thousands in a production environment, tuning performance and preparing for scalability is crucial to an API's success. In this chapter, we'll explore the full landscape of:

1. **Optimizing API performance.**
2. **Leveraging FastAPI's asynchronous superpowers.**
3. **Horizontal and vertical scaling.**
4. **Caching, load balancing, and database optimization.**
5. **Monitoring and benchmarking your API's performance in production.**
6. **Introducing Docker for deployment and scalability.**

---

1. Optimizing API Performance: Squeezing Every Bit of Speed

While FastAPI is one of the fastest Python frameworks out of the box, there are always ways to optimize further. This section covers how to fine-tune every layer of your stack, from code-level improvements to server configurations.

Minimize Blocking I/O with Async and Await

FastAPI's speed comes largely from its use of Python's asynchronous capabilities, allowing the application to handle multiple requests at once. However, to get the most out of this feature, it's important to ensure that you minimize blocking I/O operations (e.g., database queries, network requests). If you're calling a slow API synchronously, your FastAPI app will be blocked until the request completes. Always use async I/O operations for external calls.

Example: When making a call to an external API or database:

```python
import httpx

async def fetch_data():
    async with httpx.AsyncClient() as client:
        response = await client.get("https://api.example.com/data")
        return response.json()

@app.get("/data/")
async def get_data():
    return await fetch_data()
```

This ensures FastAPI can handle other requests while waiting for the external API to respond.

Use Connection Pooling

Connecting to a database for each request is expensive. Instead, reuse connections through connection pooling. SQLAlchemy, used with FastAPI, offers built-in connection pooling, which can reduce overhead significantly.

SQLAlchemy Configuration:

```
from sqlalchemy import create_engine
engine = create_engine(
    "postgresql://user:password@localhost/db",
    pool_size=20, max_overflow=10
)
```

Profile and Monitor for Bottlenecks

No optimization strategy is complete without identifying where the real bottlenecks lie. Use profiling tools such as **Py-Spy**, **cProfile**, and **memory_profiler** to find out which parts of your API are taking the longest to execute or consuming the most memory.

---

2. Asynchronous Programming – Leveraging FastAPI's Superpowers

One of FastAPI's greatest strengths is its **async** support, which allows it to handle thousands of connections efficiently. Here's why you should lean into asynchronous programming:

- **Non-blocking Calls**: With traditional (synchronous) APIs, a request that takes a long time to complete will block the server from handling other requests. In contrast, FastAPI's async capabilities allow the server to handle multiple requests concurrently.
- **Improving Throughput**: By making routes and database calls asynchronous, your API can handle more users at once, improving overall throughput.

Example: Suppose you're calling an external API to retrieve data. Here's how you can make the function non-blocking using `asyncio`:

```python
import asyncio
import httpx

async def fetch_data():
    async with httpx.AsyncClient() as client:
        response = await client.get("https://api.example.com/data")
        return response.json()

@app.get("/data/")
async def get_data():
    return await fetch_data()
```

---

3. Scaling Your API – Horizontal vs. Vertical Scaling

At some point, your API will need to scale to meet demand. There are two primary methods for scaling an API:

Vertical Scaling:

- Involves adding more resources (CPU, memory) to a single server to handle more requests.
- **Pros**: Simple and straightforward.
- **Cons**: There's a limit to how much you can scale vertically before it becomes inefficient.

Horizontal Scaling:

- Involves adding more servers to distribute the load.
- **Pros**: Highly scalable and allows for fault tolerance. Multiple instances of your API can handle requests simultaneously, especially when coupled with **load balancers**.

- **Cons**: More complex to set up, but essential for handling large-scale applications.

Tip: Use tools like **Gunicorn** with **Uvicorn workers** to distribute the load across multiple worker processes.

```
gunicorn -w 4 -k uvicorn.workers.UvicornWorker main:app
```

4. Caching – Speeding Up Your API Responses

Caching is a technique that can drastically improve the performance of your API by reducing the need for expensive computations or database queries on repeated requests. FastAPI can easily integrate caching using tools like **Redis**.

Example: Using Redis for Caching

You can cache the result of an API response so that subsequent requests can be served faster:

```python
import aioredis

redis = await aioredis.create_redis_pool("redis://localhost")

@app.get("/cached-data/")
async def get_cached_data():
    cached = await redis.get("key:data")
    if cached:
        return cached
    data = await expensive_computation()
    await redis.set("key:data", data, expire=60)
    return data
```

5. Load Balancing – Distributing the Load

As your API grows, load balancing becomes crucial to evenly distribute incoming traffic across multiple servers or instances. **Nginx** and **HAProxy** are commonly used tools to set up load balancing, ensuring that no single server is overwhelmed.

Example: Basic Nginx Load Balancer Configuration

```
upstream myapp {
    server app1.example.com;
    server app2.example.com;
}

server {
    listen 80;
    location / {
        proxy_pass http://myapp;
    }
}
```

This configuration allows requests to be distributed between `app1` and `app2`, reducing the load on individual servers and increasing fault tolerance.

---

6. Database Optimizations

Databases are often the slowest part of an API, so optimizing database interactions is key to improving overall performance:

- **Connection Pooling**: Reuse database connections to avoid the overhead of creating new ones.
- **Query Optimization**: Ensure that database queries are efficient by using indexes and avoiding N+1 query problems.

- **Read/Write Splitting**: In larger applications, use separate databases for reads and writes to reduce contention.

FastAPI pairs perfectly with **SQLAlchemy** for database operations, and tools like **pgbouncer** can help manage connection pooling for PostgreSQL databases.

---

7. Using Docker for Simplified Deployment and Scaling

As your API grows, managing dependencies and deployment across different environments can become challenging. Docker simplifies this by packaging your entire application, along with its dependencies, into lightweight, portable containers that can run consistently across development, testing, and production environments.

Basic Docker Setup for FastAPI

Let's start with a simple Docker setup to containerize your FastAPI application. With Docker, you can ensure that your application runs in a consistent environment, no matter where it's deployed.

Dockerfile:

```dockerfile
# Use an official Python runtime as the base image
FROM python:3.11-slim

# Set the working directory
WORKDIR /app

# Copy the requirements file into the container
COPY requirements.txt .

# Install the Python dependencies
RUN pip install --no-cache-dir -r requirements.txt
```

```
# Copy the FastAPI application code into the
container
COPY . .

# Expose port 8000 and start FastAPI using Uvicorn
EXPOSE 8000
CMD ["uvicorn", "main:app", "--host", "0.0.0.0", "--port", "8000"]
```

Running Your API with Docker

Once you've written your Dockerfile, build and run your containerized FastAPI app using the following commands:

1. **Build the Docker Image**:
   ```
   docker build -t fastapi-app .
   ```

2. **Run the Docker Container**:
   ```
   docker run -d -p 8000:8000 fastapi-app
   ```

Using Docker Compose for Multi-Container Applications

In production environments, your FastAPI app will likely need to interact with a database, a caching layer, or other services. **Docker Compose** simplifies managing multi-container setups, allowing you to define and run multiple services with a single command.

Here's an example `docker-compose.yml` file that runs a FastAPI app along with a PostgreSQL database:

```
version: "3.8"
services:
  fastapi:
    build: .
    ports:
```

```yaml
      - "8000:8000"
    depends_on:
      - db
    environment:
      - DATABASE_URL=postgresql://postgres:password@db:5432/mydb

  db:
    image: postgres:13
    environment:
      POSTGRES_USER: postgres
      POSTGRES_PASSWORD: password
      POSTGRES_DB: mydb
    volumes:
      - postgres_data:/var/lib/postgresql/data

volumes:
  postgres_data:
```

Conclusion: Scaling Up – Taming the API Jungle

Performance tuning and scalability are the unsung heroes of API development. It's not enough to simply build a functional API—your application needs to be fast, responsive, and capable of handling growth. By leveraging FastAPI's async capabilities, caching results, optimizing database queries, setting up load balancers, and containerizing your application with Docker, you can ensure that your API is prepared for anything the jungle throws at it.

Docker, in particular, plays a crucial role by making deployment and scaling easier than ever. By containerizing your FastAPI app and orchestrating services with Docker Compose, you ensure a consistent environment across development, testing, and production. Combined with horizontal scaling, load balancing, and database optimizations, you've built an API that's ready to handle the wild world of production-scale traffic.

By mastering these techniques, you've moved from creating a simple, functioning API to architecting a robust, scalable system capable of handling massive traffic loads—all without breaking a sweat.

Chapter 10: Automated Function Testing – Keep the Jungle Running Smoothly

When you're navigating the API jungle, it's not enough to simply build an API that works once—it has to keep working as you add new features, fix bugs, and scale your infrastructure. This is where automated function testing becomes your best guide through the wilderness.

In this chapter, we'll cover:

1. **The importance of automated testing in API development.**
2. **Setting up automated tests in FastAPI using `pytest`.**
3. **Writing comprehensive test cases for your API endpoints.**
4. **Ensuring coverage across all endpoints and scenarios.**
5. **Integration of testing into CI/CD pipelines for continuous validation.**

1. Why Automated Testing is Critical for Your API

Automated function testing is like the map you need to make it through the ever-changing jungle of API development. Without it, every change you make is a gamble—will your new feature break existing functionality? Automated tests give you the confidence to add new features without fear, knowing that the essential parts of your API are always functioning as expected.

Key benefits include:

- **Catching bugs early**: Automated tests catch issues before they make it into production, saving you time and costly rollbacks.
- **Ensuring API stability**: As your API grows, tests ensure that new changes don't introduce regressions.
- **Reducing manual effort**: With automated testing, you're no longer running through long manual checklists to verify that your API works as expected.

2. Setting Up Automated Tests with Pytest

FastAPI works seamlessly with **pytest**, one of Python's most popular testing frameworks. Let's set up a basic testing environment to get you started.

Install pytest and Test Dependencies

First, install `pytest` and `httpx` (for making requests to your API):

```
pip install pytest httpx
```

Next, create a `tests` folder in your project where all your test files will live. This will help organize your test cases.

Basic Test Structure

Inside the `tests` folder, create a file named `test_main.py` and set up a basic test to check if your API is working:

```python
from fastapi.testclient import TestClient
from main import app

client = TestClient(app)

def test_read_main():
    response = client.get("/")
    assert response.status_code == 200
    assert response.json() == {"message": "Hello World"}
```

This simple test checks whether the root / endpoint returns a 200 status code and the correct JSON response.

Running the Tests

To run your tests, use `pytest` in your terminal:

```
pytest
```

You should see the output of the tests and whether they passed or failed. If all goes well, you'll get a summary of tests that passed without any issues.

```
PS C:\Users\pat\Documents\API-ocalypse_Now\code-v2> pytest
============================= test session starts =============================
platform win32 -- Python 3.11.9, pytest-8.3.3, pluggy-1.5.0
rootdir: C:\Users\pat\Documents\API-ocalypse_Now\code-v2
plugins: anyio-4.4.0
collected 1 item

test_main.py .                                                          [100%]

============================== warnings summary ===============================
db.py:11
  C:\Users\pat\Documents\API-ocalypse_Now\code-v2\db.py:11: MovedIn20Warning: The ``declarative_base()`` f
unction is now available as sqlalchemy.orm.declarative_base(). (deprecated since: 2.0) (Background on SQLA
lchemy 2.0 at: https://sqlalche.me/e/b8d9)
    Base = declarative_base()

test_main.py::test_read_main
  C:\Users\pat\Documents\API-ocalypse_Now\code-v2\.venv\Lib\site-packages\starlette\templating.py:161: Dep
recationWarning: The `name` is not the first parameter anymore. The first parameter should be the `Request
` instance.
  Replace `TemplateResponse(name, {"request": request})` by `TemplateResponse(request, name)`.
    warnings.warn(

-- Docs: https://docs.pytest.org/en/stable/how-to/capture-warnings.html
======================== 1 passed, 2 warnings in 1.35s ========================
```

3. Writing Comprehensive Test Cases for API Endpoints

The key to automated testing is making sure you have comprehensive test coverage for your API. Let's break this down into the types of tests you should write:

Testing CRUD Operations

For each endpoint in your API, you'll want to write tests that cover all CRUD operations (Create, Read, Update, Delete). Here's an example of how you might write tests for a **POST** request to add an animal to your database:

```python
def test_create_animal():
    response = client.post(
        "/animals/",
        json={"name": "Lion", "species": "Panthera leo", "age": 5},
    )
    assert response.status_code == 200
    assert response.json()["message"] == "Added Lion the Panthera leo to the database."
```

Edge Case Testing

Don't forget to test edge cases! What happens if the user submits invalid data? How does your API handle it? Here's an example of an edge case test that checks whether the API rejects an invalid age value (based on the Pydantic validation rules you implemented):

```python
def test_create_animal_invalid_age():
    response = client.post(
        "/animals/",
        json={"name": "Tiger", "species": "Panthera tigris", "age": -1},
    )
    assert response.status_code == 422
```

This test ensures that the age field validation works and rejects negative numbers.

---

4. Ensuring Coverage Across All Endpoints and Scenarios

Testing your API's happy paths is important, but equally important is testing what happens when things go wrong. Your automated tests should cover:

- **Successful requests**: The API behaves as expected under normal conditions.
- **Error handling**: The API returns appropriate error codes (like 400 Bad Request or 404 Not Found) for invalid requests.
- **Edge cases**: Test the boundaries of what your API accepts and rejects.

A good rule of thumb is to aim for **80% test coverage** for your endpoints, ensuring you've tested both positive and negative scenarios.

Test Coverage Tools

You can integrate tools like **coverage.py** to measure the effectiveness of your tests. Here's how to install it:

```
pip install coverage
```

Then, run your tests with coverage reporting:

```
coverage run -m pytest
coverage report
```

```
PS C:\Users\pat\Documents\API-ocalypse_Now\code-v2> coverage report
Name              Stmts   Miss  Cover
-----------------------------------
db.py                14      0   100%
main.py              93     44    53%
model.py              5      0   100%
test_main.py          7      0   100%
-----------------------------------
TOTAL               119     44    63%
```

5. Continuous Integration and Testing

Once you have a solid test suite in place, the next step is integrating testing into your CI/CD pipeline. Automated tests should run every time code is committed to the repository, ensuring no code changes break your API.

GitHub Actions for Testing

Here's an example workflow file for running tests automatically using **GitHub Actions**:

```
name: CI

on:
  push:
    branches:
      - main

jobs:
  test:
    runs-on: ubuntu-latest
    steps:
```

```yaml
- name: Checkout code
  uses: actions/checkout@v2

- name: Set up Python
  uses: actions/setup-python@v2
  with:
    python-version: 3.11

- name: Install dependencies
  run: pip install -r requirements.txt

- name: Run tests
  run: pytest
```

With this configuration, every time you push new code to the `main` branch, GitHub Actions will run your tests automatically. This ensures that your API stays bug-free as new features are added.

Conclusion: Automated Testing is Your Safety Net

In the jungle of API development, automated testing is your safety net. It ensures that your API not only works today but continues to work as you add new features and scale up. By incorporating tests for every endpoint, testing edge cases, and integrating testing into your CI/CD pipeline, you can confidently deploy your API knowing that everything is running smoothly.

Think of testing as your early warning system. The more comprehensive your tests, the less likely you are to encounter critical issues in production. In short: **Automated function testing keeps your API jungle running smoothly, no matter how wild things get.**

Chapter 11: Securing Your API – Beyond the Basics

In an age where data breaches are front-page news, ensuring the security of your API is crucial. While we've covered the basics of JWT-based authentication, true API security involves much more. This chapter dives deeper into advanced security practices, exploring how to protect your API from common threats and ensure your users' data stays safe.

1. OAuth2 for Advanced Authentication

OAuth2 is the industry standard for access delegation, allowing users to grant third-party services access to their information without sharing their credentials. Popular services like Google, Facebook, and GitHub use OAuth2 to authenticate users across platforms.

How OAuth2 Works

At its core, OAuth2 is about granting limited access to resources on behalf of a user. Instead of directly sharing credentials (like passwords), OAuth2 uses **tokens** to grant access. Here's a simplified flow:

1. The user logs in via a third-party OAuth2 provider (e.g., Google).
2. The third-party provider generates a **token**.
3. Your application uses that token to access the user's data from the third-party service (without handling their password).

OAuth2 in FastAPI

To integrate OAuth2 into your FastAPI app, you can use FastAPI's built-in support for OAuth2 with **OAuth2PasswordBearer**. This process allows you to set up token-based authentication for endpoints. However, for more complex OAuth flows (like those involving third-party services), you might need to use libraries like `authlib`.

Here's an example of a basic OAuth2 setup using password authentication:

```python
from fastapi import FastAPI, Depends, HTTPException, status
from fastapi.security import OAuth2PasswordBearer

app = FastAPI()

oauth2_scheme = OAuth2PasswordBearer(tokenUrl="token")

@app.get("/users/me")
async def read_users_me(token: str = Depends(oauth2_scheme)):
    if not token:
        raise HTTPException(status_code=status.HTTP_401_UNAUTHORIZED, detail="Invalid token")
    return {"token": token}
```

This is just a small piece of the puzzle. For integrating OAuth2 with providers like Google, you'd need to handle the complete flow, including client and secret management.

2. Rate Limiting to Prevent Abuse

In any public-facing API, there's always the risk of abuse. One way to mitigate this is through **rate limiting**, which restricts how many requests a client can make within a specified time frame.

This can help protect against **DDoS attacks** and prevent any single user from overwhelming your system.

Implementing Rate Limiting with FastAPI

One way to add rate limiting to your FastAPI app is by using the `slowapi` library, which is built on top of Flask-Limiter. This allows you to define specific rate limits for endpoints:

```
from fastapi import FastAPI
from slowapi import Limiter
from slowapi.util import get_remote_address

limiter = Limiter(key_func=get_remote_address)

app = FastAPI()

@app.get("/items")
@limiter.limit("5 per minute")
def read_items():
    return {"message": "Limited to 5 requests per minute"}
```

This simple example limits users to 5 requests per minute to the `/items` endpoint. You can customize rate limits for specific routes or even user roles.

3. API Keys for External Integrations

Many APIs rely on external integrations, where you might need to expose certain endpoints to third-party services. **API keys** are a common way to secure these integrations, ensuring only authorized applications can access your API.

How API Keys Work

API keys are essentially a unique identifier that third-party services send with each request to your API. On your end, you validate the key and allow or deny access based on its validity.

Implementing API Key Authentication in FastAPI

FastAPI makes it easy to implement API key-based security. You can use dependencies to validate an API key passed via headers or query parameters.

```python
from fastapi import FastAPI, Depends, HTTPException

app = FastAPI()

def get_api_key(api_key: str):
    if api_key != "supersecretapikey":
        raise HTTPException(status_code=403, detail="Invalid API key")
    return api_key

@app.get("/secure-data")
async def secure_data(api_key: str = Depends(get_api_key)):
    return {"data": "Here's the secure data"}
```

This basic example checks if the incoming API key is valid and only allows access if it matches.

4. Encrypting Sensitive Data

Sensitive data such as passwords, personal information, and tokens should never be transmitted in plaintext. Using encryption ensures that even if data is intercepted, it cannot be read by unauthorized parties.

Using HTTPS

Ensure that all traffic to and from your API is encrypted using **HTTPS**. This can be done by configuring your web server (e.g., Nginx or Apache) to enforce HTTPS. Many platforms like AWS, Azure, and Google Cloud make this easy with automated SSL certificate management.

Encrypting Data at Rest

Beyond just encrypting data in transit (using HTTPS), consider encrypting sensitive data at rest. For example, encrypt passwords before storing them in your database using libraries like **bcrypt** or **argon2**.

```
from passlib.context import CryptContext

pwd_context = CryptContext(schemes=["bcrypt"], deprecated="auto")

def verify_password(plain_password, hashed_password):
    return pwd_context.verify(plain_password, hashed_password)

def get_password_hash(password):
    return pwd_context.hash(password)
```

In this example, passwords are hashed before being stored in the database, ensuring that even if your database is compromised, passwords remain protected.

5. Auditing and Logging for Security

Auditing and logging play a crucial role in identifying and preventing security incidents. By keeping track of API usage, you can detect suspicious patterns that may indicate an attempted breach.

Implementing Audit Logs

Audit logs should record every request, including metadata like the requester's IP address, endpoint accessed, and any authentication attempts. FastAPI makes this straightforward by using middleware to capture logging information.

```python
import logging
from fastapi import FastAPI, Request

logging.basicConfig(filename="audit.log",
level=logging.INFO)

app = FastAPI()

@app.middleware("http")
async def log_requests(request: Request, call_next):
    logging.info(f"Request from {request.client.host} to {request.url}")
    response = await call_next(request)
    return response
```

This example logs each incoming request, helping you track usage and detect abnormalities.

Tracking Failed Login Attempts

Another useful audit feature is tracking failed authentication attempts. This can help identify brute-force attacks where a malicious actor tries to guess user credentials.

```python
@app.post("/login")
async def login(username: str, password: str):
    if not verify_credentials(username, password):
        logging.warning(f"Failed login attempt for {username}")
        raise HTTPException(status_code=401, detail="Invalid credentials")
    return {"message": "Login successful"}
```

By logging failed login attempts, you can take action when you notice repeated failures from a single source.

Conclusion: Securing Your API Beyond Authentication

While JWT authentication provides a solid foundation for securing your API, true security goes far beyond authentication. By implementing advanced features like OAuth2, rate limiting, API key validation, encryption, and auditing, you can protect your API against the ever-growing landscape of threats.

This chapter provides a comprehensive toolkit for API security, allowing you to fortify your API and sleep soundly knowing your application is well-protected from common attack vectors. After all, securing your API is like setting up strong defenses in the jungle—without them, you're leaving your treasures vulnerable.

Chapter 12: API Documentation Best Practices

In the world of APIs, documentation is often the unsung hero. While building a highly functional and scalable API is essential, none of it matters if your users can't figure out how to use it. Comprehensive and clear documentation helps developers integrate and work with your API effortlessly. With FastAPI, much of this work is done for you automatically, but there are ways to customize and extend documentation to ensure it's as effective as possible.

1. Automatic Documentation with Swagger and ReDoc

FastAPI's automatic generation of OpenAPI documentation via Swagger is a massive time-saver. Every time you create an endpoint, FastAPI automatically updates your API's documentation to reflect the new or changed routes, request parameters, and expected responses.

Swagger UI

The default documentation interface in FastAPI is **Swagger UI**, a visually appealing and interactive tool that allows developers to try out API calls directly from their browser. It's great for quickly testing endpoints and validating responses.

To access the Swagger documentation for your FastAPI app, simply navigate to `/docs` on your running API:

```
http://127.0.0.1:8000/docs
```

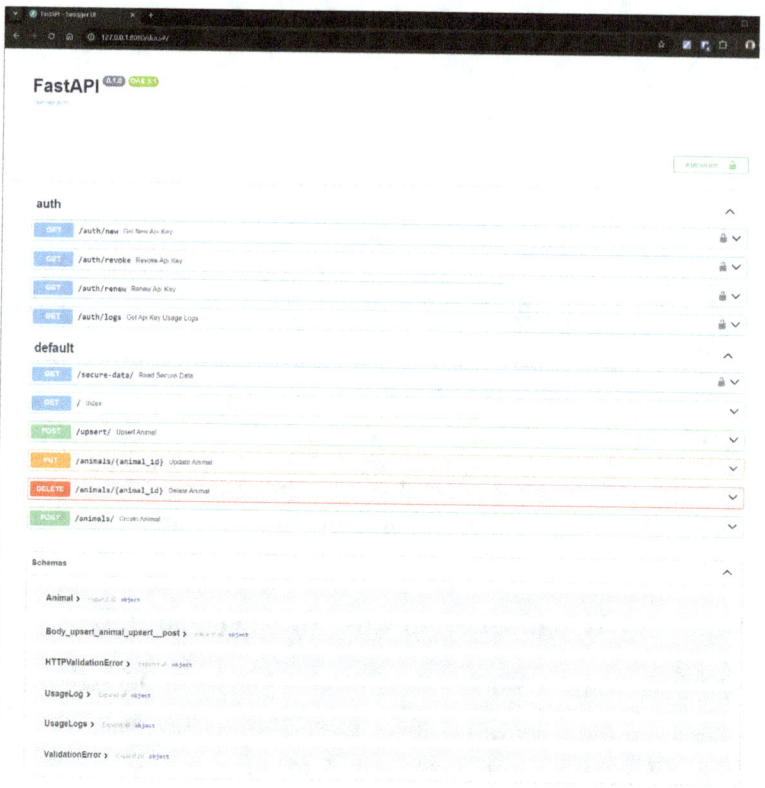

ReDoc

ReDoc provides a more structured and professional-looking UI for API documentation. FastAPI includes a ReDoc-generated documentation page at `/redoc`, which is also based on your OpenAPI schema. ReDoc presents your API in a well-organized format, making it easy for users to explore and understand its structure.

To access ReDoc:

```
http://127.0.0.1:8000/redoc
```

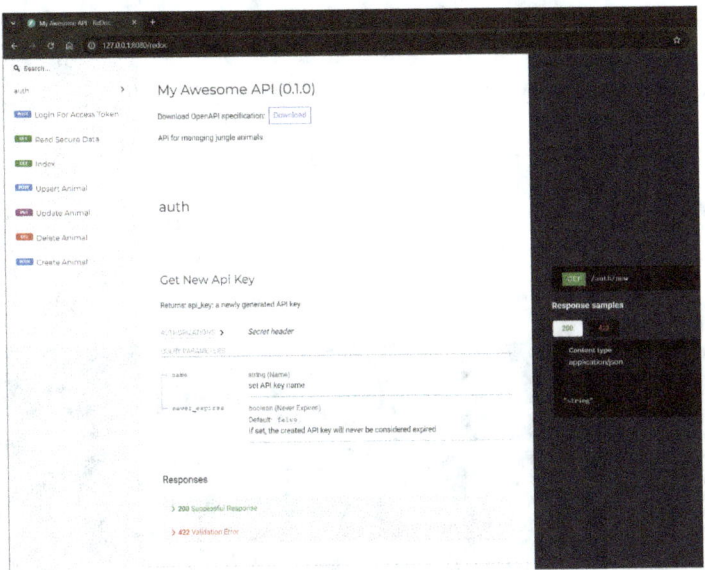

2. Customizing the Documentation

While FastAPI's automatic documentation generation is incredibly helpful, there are cases where you'll want to provide more context or customize the appearance of the documentation.

Adding Descriptions to Your Endpoints

You can add detailed descriptions to your API endpoints to give users a better understanding of what each endpoint does, expected inputs, and potential responses. FastAPI allows you to do this by passing a `description` parameter to your route decorators.

```
@app.get("/items", description="Retrieve a list of
all available items.")
def get_items():
    return {"items": ["item1", "item2"]}
```

Descriptions like these are automatically included in your Swagger and ReDoc docs, improving the clarity of your API.

Using Markdown for Richer Documentation

FastAPI supports using **Markdown** in your descriptions. This means you can add formatted text, bullet points, and even code blocks to make your documentation richer and more readable.

```
@app.get(
    "/users/{user_id}",
    description="""
        This endpoint retrieves a user by their unique ID.

        **Parameters:**
        - `user_id`: The unique identifier for the user.

        **Responses:**
        - `200`: User details returned successfully.
        - `404`: User not found.
    """
)
def read_user(user_id: int):
    return {"user_id": user_id}
```

By using Markdown, you can make your documentation much more informative and visually appealing.

Customizing Tags and Metadata

Tags allow you to group your endpoints by functionality. For example, you can group all authentication-related endpoints under the "Auth" tag and all item-related endpoints under "Items." Tags make it easier for developers to find the information they need in your API.

```
@app.get("/items", tags=["Items"])
def get_items():
    return {"items": ["item1", "item2"]}
```

You can also add metadata like version numbers, contact information, and terms of service to your API's OpenAPI schema using FastAPI's `openapi_tags` and `openapi_info` settings.

3. Versioning Your API

As your API evolves, you'll inevitably make changes that might not be backward-compatible. This is where **API versioning** comes into play. Versioning allows you to maintain different versions of your API simultaneously, so older clients aren't affected by breaking changes.

URL-Based Versioning

One common approach to versioning is to include the version number in the URL path. This way, different versions of the API are accessible via different paths.

```
@app.get("/v1/items")
def get_items_v1():
    return {"items": ["item1", "item2"]}

@app.get("/v2/items")
def get_items_v2():
    return {"items": ["itemA", "itemB"]}
```

In this example, both versions of the API are available, and clients can choose which version to use.

Header-Based Versioning

Another approach is to use request headers to specify the API version. This keeps the URL clean and allows clients to choose the version via headers like `Accept-Version`.

```
@app.get("/items")
def get_items(version: str = Header(None)):
    if version == "v1":
        return {"items": ["item1", "item2"]}
    elif version == "v2":
        return {"items": ["itemA", "itemB"]}
```

Each approach has its pros and cons, and the best choice depends on your API's needs and your clients' requirements.

4. Generating Client SDKs from OpenAPI

Once you have well-documented APIs, generating client libraries in various programming languages becomes easy using the OpenAPI schema. These client libraries allow developers to interact with your API without having to write boilerplate code.

Using Swagger Codegen

Swagger Codegen is a tool that takes your OpenAPI schema and generates client SDKs in languages like Python, JavaScript, TypeScript, and more. To generate a client library for your API, you can use the following command:

```bash
swagger-codegen generate -i http://127.0.0.1:8000/openapi.json -l python -o ./client
```

This command will generate a Python client for your FastAPI app, which developers can use to easily integrate with your API.

5. Best Practices for Writing API Documentation

Good documentation isn't just about listing endpoints and parameters—it's about providing clear and useful information that helps developers use your API effectively. Here are some best practices for writing API documentation:

- **Be clear and concise**: Avoid jargon and technical complexity wherever possible. Your documentation should be easy to read and understand.
- **Provide examples**: Real-world examples of API requests and responses can help users quickly understand how to interact with your API.
- **Document edge cases and errors**: Be sure to document how your API handles error cases and what users can expect when something goes wrong. Include all possible HTTP status codes and their meanings.
- **Keep it up-to-date**: As your API evolves, it's crucial to keep the documentation in sync with the current state of the API. FastAPI helps automate this, but any custom documentation should be regularly updated.

Conclusion: Building Great Documentation

Great API documentation can mean the difference between a successful API that developers love to use and one that's confusing and underutilized. FastAPI's built-in tools for generating OpenAPI-based docs, combined with customization and best practices, make it easy to create documentation that's not only accurate but also clear and easy to navigate.

By adding detailed descriptions, rich Markdown formatting, versioning strategies, and client SDK generation, you can ensure that your API documentation is as polished as the API itself. After all, a well-documented API is a developer's best friend.

Chapter 13: Deploying Your API – From Local to Cloud

Building a local API is just the first step. To make your API accessible to users worldwide, you need to deploy it to a server or a cloud platform. In this chapter, we'll explore different deployment strategies and best practices for deploying FastAPI applications from your local environment to the cloud.

1. Preparing Your API for Deployment

Before deploying your API, it's important to ensure that it's production-ready. Here are a few things to keep in mind:

- **Environment Variables**: Avoid hardcoding sensitive information (e.g., API keys, database URLs) into your code. Instead, use environment variables and a `.env` file to store these credentials securely.
- **Production Server Configuration**: FastAPI uses Uvicorn for development, but for production, you should use a more robust server configuration like **Gunicorn** with **Uvicorn workers**.

Example: Running Uvicorn with Gunicorn for production:

```
gunicorn -w 4 -k uvicorn.workers.UvicornWorker main:app
```

This command starts your FastAPI app with 4 worker processes, improving performance and fault tolerance.

2. Deploying to AWS (Amazon Web Services)

AWS is one of the most popular cloud platforms for deploying APIs. You can use a variety of services such as **EC2** for virtual machines, **Elastic Beanstalk** for simplified deployment, or **Lambda** for serverless deployment.

Deploying FastAPI on EC2

To deploy your API on AWS EC2, follow these steps:

1. **Launch an EC2 instance**: Choose an Amazon Linux or Ubuntu server and configure the instance with enough CPU and memory to handle your expected traffic.
2. **Install dependencies**: Once your EC2 instance is running, SSH into it and install Python, FastAPI, Uvicorn, and any other dependencies using `pip`.
3. **Configure your firewall**: Make sure your EC2 security groups allow incoming traffic on port 80 (HTTP) and 443 (HTTPS) if using SSL.
4. **Set up Gunicorn and Nginx**: Use Gunicorn to serve your FastAPI app and Nginx as a reverse proxy to manage traffic and handle SSL.

Deploying with AWS Elastic Beanstalk

Elastic Beanstalk simplifies the deployment process by automatically managing scaling, load balancing, and server configurations for you. Simply create a **Python environment** in Elastic Beanstalk, upload your project, and AWS will handle the rest.

1. Install the **Elastic Beanstalk CLI** and initialize your project:

```
eb init
```

2. Deploy the application using:

```
eb create
```

3. Elastic Beanstalk will automatically handle scaling, logging, and monitoring for your FastAPI app.

3. Deploying to Azure

Microsoft Azure offers a variety of services for deploying web apps, including **App Service** and **Azure Kubernetes Service (AKS)**.

Deploying with Azure App Service

Azure App Service is a fully managed platform for building, deploying, and scaling web apps. It allows you to deploy your FastAPI app with just a few clicks.

1. **Create an App Service**: In the Azure portal, create a new **App Service** and select the runtime stack (e.g., Python 3.8).
2. **Deploy your FastAPI app**: You can use **Git** or **Azure CLI** to deploy your app directly from your local machine or repository. For example, using the Azure CLI:

```
az webapp up --name MyFastAPIApp --resource-group MyResourceGroup --plan MyAppServicePlan
```

Azure App Service provides built-in autoscaling, logging, and SSL support, making it an ideal solution for deploying FastAPI applications.

4. Deploying to Google Cloud Platform (GCP)

Google Cloud Platform (GCP) offers several options for deploying APIs, including **Compute Engine**, **App Engine**, and **Cloud Run**.

Deploying with Google Cloud Run (Serverless)

Google Cloud Run is a serverless platform that automatically scales your API in response to traffic. It's a great option for applications with unpredictable traffic patterns.

1. **Containerize your FastAPI app**: Cloud Run uses containers, so first, create a `Dockerfile` for your FastAPI app if you haven't already.
2. **Build and deploy the container**: Use **gcloud** to build and deploy your containerized app to Cloud Run:

```
gcloud builds submit --tag gcr.io/[PROJECT-ID]/fastapi-app
gcloud run deploy --image gcr.io/[PROJECT-ID]/fastapi-app --platform managed
```

3. **Scale automatically**: Cloud Run automatically scales your app up or down based on demand, without you having to manage servers.

---

5. Serverless Deployment with AWS Lambda

For lightweight APIs or microservices, **AWS Lambda** offers a serverless solution that automatically scales and only charges you for the time your code runs. With **API Gateway**, you can expose your FastAPI app as an API without managing infrastructure.

Deploying FastAPI to AWS Lambda

1. **Package your FastAPI app with Zappa**: Zappa is a framework that makes it easy to deploy Python applications to Lambda. Install Zappa and configure it for your app:

   ```
   pip install zappa
   zappa init
   zappa deploy
   ```

2. **Automatic scaling**: Lambda automatically scales based on the number of incoming requests. You don't need to worry about server management, and you only pay for the time your API spends processing requests.

---

6. Automating Deployment with CI/CD

A Continuous Integration and Continuous Deployment (CI/CD) pipeline automates the deployment of your API whenever you push changes to your repository. Tools like **GitHub Actions**, **Travis CI**, and **Jenkins** make it easy to set up automated deployment pipelines.

Example: CI/CD with GitHub Actions

Here's a simple GitHub Actions workflow that automatically deploys your FastAPI app to an AWS EC2 instance every time you push to the `main` branch:

```
name: CI/CD Pipeline

on:
  push:
    branches:
      - main
```

```yaml
jobs:
  deploy:
    runs-on: ubuntu-latest
    steps:
    - name: Checkout Code
      uses: actions/checkout@v2
    - name: Set up Python
      uses: actions/setup-python@v2
      with:
        python-version: 3.11
    - name: Install Dependencies
      run: pip install -r requirements.txt
    - name: Deploy to EC2
      run: |
        scp -i ~/.ssh/id_rsa -r . ubuntu@ec2-instance:/var/www/myapp
        ssh -i ~/.ssh/id_rsa ubuntu@ec2-instance 'sudo systemctl restart gunicorn'
```

With this setup, every code push triggers an automated deployment to your EC2 instance.

Conclusion: From Local to Cloud

Deploying your FastAPI API from a local environment to the cloud requires careful planning, but it opens up a world of possibilities. Whether you choose AWS, Azure, or Google Cloud, each platform offers tools for scaling, monitoring, and managing your API. Serverless options like AWS Lambda and Google Cloud Run allow you to run your API with minimal infrastructure management, while EC2 and App Service offer more control over your environment.

By automating your deployment process with CI/CD pipelines, you can ensure that every code change is smoothly and reliably deployed to production. Now that you know how to deploy, your API is ready to conquer the cloud!

Chapter 14: Monitoring and Observability in FastAPI

Building and deploying an API is just the beginning. Once your API is live, monitoring its health, performance, and behavior is essential to maintaining a smooth user experience. This chapter explores how to monitor your FastAPI application, measure key performance metrics, and set up alerts when something goes wrong. We'll look at tools like **Prometheus**, **Grafana**, and structured logging to help ensure your API is running smoothly.

1. The Importance of Observability

Observability refers to the ability to understand the internal state of a system by examining its outputs, such as logs, metrics, and traces. It helps you detect problems early, improve performance, and ensure uptime.

- **Monitoring**: Tracking the health and performance of your API to detect issues in real-time.
- **Metrics**: Collecting key performance indicators (e.g., request throughput, latency, error rates).
- **Logging**: Capturing logs of system activity to identify abnormal patterns and errors.
- **Tracing**: Tracking the journey of a request through your system to pinpoint performance bottlenecks.

These components together give you insight into your API's operation and behavior, allowing you to catch and resolve issues before they affect users.

---

2. Logging Best Practices

Logs are crucial for understanding what's happening inside your API at any given moment. Proper logging allows you to track incoming requests, errors, and unusual behavior. FastAPI works well with Python's standard logging module, but you can also integrate more advanced logging tools.

Using Loguru for Structured Logging

Loguru is a Python library that simplifies logging and provides structured, readable log output. Here's how you can set it up in FastAPI:

```python
from loguru import logger
from fastapi import FastAPI

app = FastAPI()

@app.middleware("http")
async def log_requests(request, call_next):
    logger.info(f"Incoming request: {request.method} {request.url}")
    response = await call_next(request)
    logger.info(f"Response status: {response.status_code}")
    return response
```

This middleware logs every incoming request and outgoing response, helping you track the lifecycle of each API call. You can also log additional information such as request payloads, response times, and error messages.

Log Levels

Make sure to use appropriate log levels (INFO, WARNING, ERROR, etc.) to differentiate between normal operations and critical issues. This helps you filter through logs quickly to find the root cause of a problem.

```
logger.warning("Potential issue detected!")
logger.error("Critical failure occurred!")
```

---

3. Metrics and Monitoring with Prometheus

While logs provide detailed information about specific events, metrics give you a broader view of your API's health and performance. Metrics like request latency, error rates, and request throughput are essential for monitoring your API over time.

Prometheus is an open-source monitoring tool designed to collect and store time-series data. You can integrate Prometheus with FastAPI to monitor key performance metrics.

Setting Up Prometheus with FastAPI

You can use the **prometheus-client** library to expose metrics for your FastAPI app. First, install the library:

```
pip install prometheus-client
```

Then, create a metrics endpoint that Prometheus can scrape:

```
from fastapi import FastAPI
from prometheus_client import Counter, Summary, make_asgi_app

app = FastAPI()

# Create some Prometheus metrics
```

```python
REQUEST_COUNT = Counter("request_count", "Total
number of requests")
REQUEST_LATENCY = Summary("request_latency_seconds",
"Latency of requests in seconds")

@app.middleware("http")
async def monitor_requests(request, call_next):
    REQUEST_COUNT.inc()    # Increment the request counter
    with REQUEST_LATENCY.time():   # Track the request latency
        response = await call_next(request)
    return response

# Expose Prometheus metrics endpoint
metrics_app = make_asgi_app()
app.mount("/metrics", metrics_app)
```

Prometheus can scrape the `/metrics` endpoint at regular intervals to collect data.

Visualizing Metrics with Grafana

Once Prometheus is collecting metrics, you can visualize them using **Grafana**. Grafana allows you to create dashboards with graphs, charts, and alerts based on your metrics. You can set up a dashboard that tracks request rates, response times, and error rates in real-time, giving you immediate insight into your API's health.

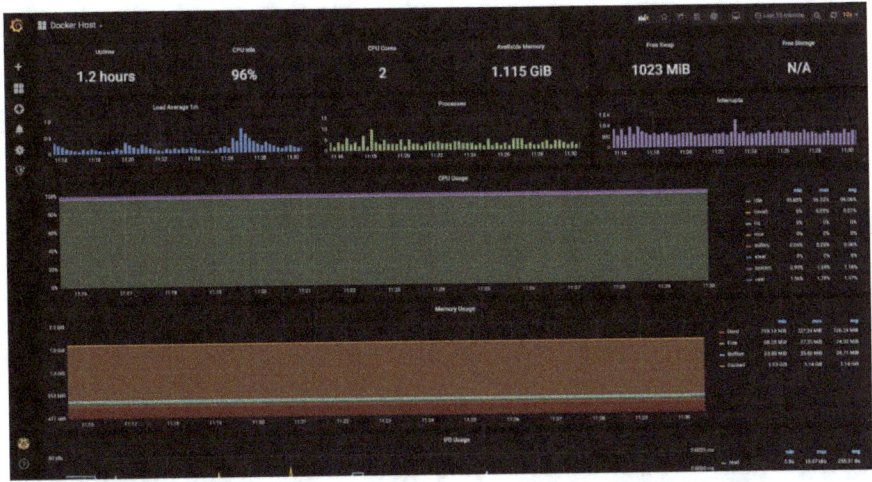

4. Health Checks and Alerting

Health checks provide a way to monitor the status of your API's dependencies (e.g., databases, external services) and ensure they're functioning correctly. If any dependencies fail, the health check will return a failure status, allowing you to detect and fix issues quickly.

Implementing Health Check Endpoints

You can create a simple health check endpoint in FastAPI that checks the status of your database connection or any other critical service:

```python
from fastapi import FastAPI
from sqlalchemy.orm import Session

app = FastAPI()

@app.get("/health")
async def health_check(db: Session):
    try:
```

```
        db.execute("SELECT 1")  # A simple query to
check the database connection
        return {"status": "healthy"}
    except:
        return {"status": "unhealthy"}
```

This endpoint returns `{"status": "healthy"}` if the database is reachable and `{"status": "unhealthy"}` if it isn't. You can extend this to check other dependencies like external APIs or cache services.

Setting Up Alerts

Alerts notify you when something goes wrong. Using tools like **Prometheus Alertmanager** or Grafana, you can set up alerts that trigger based on specific conditions (e.g., error rate exceeds a certain threshold, health check fails). These alerts can send notifications via email, Slack, or PagerDuty.

Example alert rules in Prometheus might look like this:

```
groups:
  - name: api_alerts
    rules:
      - alert: HighErrorRate
        expr: rate(request_errors_total[5m]) > 0.1
        for: 10m
        labels:
          severity: critical
        annotations:
          summary: "High error rate detected"
```

This alert rule triggers if more than 10% of requests return an error in a 5-minute window.

Conclusion: Monitoring for a Healthy API

Monitoring and observability are key to ensuring that your FastAPI application performs well in production and can quickly recover from issues. By setting up structured logging, tracking key metrics with Prometheus, and visualizing your API's performance with Grafana, you can stay on top of your API's health.

Health checks and alerts provide early warnings of problems, allowing you to fix issues before they affect your users. In short, monitoring and observability ensure that your API continues running smoothly, even in the unpredictable jungle of production environments.

Chapter 15: Real-Time Features with WebSockets

In the API world, many applications require real-time updates and two-way communication between the client and the server. Whether it's notifications, live chat applications, or stock price updates, real-time capabilities bring a dynamic and responsive user experience. This is where **WebSockets** come into play, providing an efficient way to build real-time features with FastAPI.

In this chapter, we'll explore:

1. **What WebSockets are and why you should use them.**
2. **How to set up a WebSocket endpoint in FastAPI.**
3. **Building real-time features with WebSockets.**
4. **Scaling WebSockets in production.**

---

1. Introduction to WebSockets

Unlike traditional HTTP, which operates on a request-response model, **WebSockets** enable persistent, two-way communication between the client and the server. Once a WebSocket connection is established, both the client and server can send and receive data at any time, without the need for multiple HTTP requests.

This makes WebSockets perfect for use cases like:

- **Live updates**: Stock prices, sports scores, news feeds, or game state updates.

- **Real-time messaging**: Chat apps or collaborative tools where immediate data exchange is crucial.
- **Notifications**: Push notifications sent in real time when important events occur.

WebSocket vs. HTTP

The traditional HTTP model requires the client to repeatedly send requests to the server (polling) to check for updates. WebSockets, on the other hand, maintain an open connection, allowing the server to push updates to the client as soon as they happen, without the need for polling.

---

2. Setting Up WebSockets in FastAPI

FastAPI provides built-in support for WebSockets, making it simple to set up real-time communication. Let's start with a basic WebSocket endpoint in FastAPI.

Basic WebSocket Endpoint

In this example, we'll set up a WebSocket endpoint that allows clients to connect, send messages, and receive a response from the server:

```python
from fastapi import FastAPI, WebSocket

app = FastAPI()

@app.websocket("/ws")
async def websocket_endpoint(websocket: WebSocket):
    await websocket.accept()  # Accept the WebSocket connection
    while True:
        data = await websocket.receive_text()  # Receive a message from the client
        await websocket.send_text(f"Message received: {data}")  # Send a response back
```

When a client connects to /ws, a WebSocket connection is established. The client can send messages, and the server will respond with a confirmation. This is the foundation for building real-time features like live chats or notifications.

---

3. Real-Time Features with WebSockets

Once the WebSocket connection is established, the possibilities are endless. Let's explore some practical use cases.

Example 1: Real-Time Chat Application

Imagine you're building a simple chat app where users can send messages to a server, and the server relays these messages to all connected users.

Here's how you could build a basic real-time chat with WebSockets:

```python
from fastapi import FastAPI, WebSocket
from typing import List

app = FastAPI()

active_connections: List[WebSocket] = []

async def broadcast_message(message: str):
    for connection in active_connections:
        await connection.send_text(message)

@app.websocket("/chat")
async def chat(websocket: WebSocket):
    await websocket.accept()
    active_connections.append(websocket)
    try:
        while True:
            data = await websocket.receive_text()
            await broadcast_message(f"User said: {data}")
```

```
except Exception:
    active_connections.remove(websocket)
```

In this example:

- Each new connection is added to the `active_connections` list.
- When a message is received, it's broadcasted to all connected users.
- If the connection closes or fails, it's removed from the list of active connections.

Example 2: Real-Time Notifications

WebSockets can also be used for sending real-time notifications to users, such as system alerts, order updates, or breaking news.

Here's an example of a server sending push notifications to clients in real-time:

```
from fastapi import FastAPI, WebSocket
import asyncio

app = FastAPI()

@app.websocket("/notifications")
async def notifications(websocket: WebSocket):
    await websocket.accept()
    while True:
        await asyncio.sleep(10)  # Simulate a notification being triggered
        await websocket.send_text("You've got a new notification!")
```

Every 10 seconds, a notification is pushed to the connected client. This simulates a real-time notification system where users receive updates without needing to refresh or re-request information.

4. Scaling WebSockets in Production

While WebSockets are great for real-time communication, they come with challenges, particularly when scaling. In a production environment with many users, you'll need to handle multiple WebSocket connections simultaneously and efficiently.

Handling Multiple Connections

As the number of users grows, so does the number of WebSocket connections. FastAPI, running on **Uvicorn**, supports asynchronous communication, which helps handle a large number of concurrent connections. However, you might need additional tools to scale effectively.

Using Redis Pub/Sub for WebSocket Scalability

In a distributed system with multiple servers, you'll need a way to broadcast messages across all servers so that every WebSocket connection receives the same data. **Redis Pub/Sub** is commonly used to manage this by publishing messages to a Redis channel, which all connected servers can subscribe to.

Here's how you can integrate Redis Pub/Sub to scale WebSocket broadcasts across multiple servers:

```python
import aioredis
from fastapi import FastAPI, WebSocket
from typing import List

app = FastAPI()

redis = await aioredis.create_redis_pool("redis://localhost")

async def publish_message(channel: str, message: str):
    await redis.publish(channel, message)
```

```
async def subscribe_messages(channel: str):
    (channel,) = await redis.subscribe(channel)
    while await channel.wait_message():
        message = await channel.get(encoding="utf-8")
        print(f"Received message: {message}")

@app.websocket("/ws")
async def websocket_endpoint(websocket: WebSocket):
    await websocket.accept()
    await publish_message("chat_channel", "User connected!")
    await websocket.close()
```

In this setup:

- **Publishing**: A message is published to a Redis channel (chat_channel), and all servers subscribed to that channel receive the message.
- **Subscribing**: Each server listens for new messages on the channel and can broadcast them to its WebSocket clients.

This approach allows you to horizontally scale your WebSocket servers by adding more instances without losing the ability to broadcast messages to all connected clients.

Conclusion: Bringing Real-Time Features to Life

WebSockets open up a world of possibilities for real-time communication in your API. Whether you're building a live chat application, sending real-time notifications, or delivering stock updates, WebSockets provide a fast, efficient, and scalable solution.

In production, handling multiple connections and scaling WebSockets across servers requires thoughtful architecture, but tools like Redis Pub/Sub make it easier to scale without losing performance. With FastAPI's WebSocket support, you can build dynamic, real-time APIs that keep your users engaged and responsive to new data.

Chapter 16: Creating a Front-end for Your API

While FastAPI excels as a back-end framework, many APIs require a front-end to interact with the back-end and provide users with a complete experience. In this chapter, we'll explore how to build a simple front-end that consumes your FastAPI API. By creating a front-end, you'll offer users a more intuitive way to interact with your API and complete the full-stack development experience.

In this chapter, we'll cover:

1. **Choosing a Front-end Framework (React, Vue, or Jinja2).**
2. **Building a Simple Front-end with React.**
3. **Connecting the Front-end to Your FastAPI API.**
4. **Deploying the Full-Stack Application.**

---

1. Choosing a Front-end Framework

There are various ways to build a front-end for your FastAPI application, depending on your project's goals and complexity. Here are three popular options:

- **React**: A JavaScript library for building user interfaces. React is a favorite for many developers because of its reusable components and strong community support.

- **Vue**: A lightweight, progressive JavaScript framework that's easy to integrate into existing projects. It's known for being approachable and versatile.
- **Jinja2 (Server-Side Rendering)**: If you prefer server-side rendering and want to avoid client-side frameworks, Jinja2 is a great option. FastAPI supports Jinja2 templating, allowing you to render dynamic HTML pages from your Python code.

For this chapter, we'll focus on **React** because of its popularity and ease of use. However, the concepts discussed here can be easily adapted to Vue or Jinja2.

2. Building a Simple Front-end with React

React allows you to create components that represent pieces of your user interface. For example, you can create components for displaying lists, forms, and buttons, then compose them together to create a complete web page.

Setting Up a React Project

To start, you need to set up a basic React project. Using **Create React App**, you can quickly scaffold a React application:

```
npx create-react-app fastapi-frontend
cd fastapi-frontend
npm start
```

This will set up a new React project and start a development server on `http://localhost:3000`. Now, you're ready to start building your front-end.

Creating a Simple Component

Let's build a simple component that fetches data from your FastAPI API and displays it. First, update the `App.js` file to fetch data from your API and render it in the browser.

```jsx
import React, { useEffect, useState } from "react";

function App() {
  const [items, setItems] = useState([]);

  useEffect(() => {
    fetch("http://127.0.0.1:8000/items")
      .then((response) => response.json())
      .then((data) => setItems(data.items));
  }, []);

  return (
    <div>
      <h1>Items List</h1>
      <ul>
        {items.map((item, index) => (
          <li key={index}>{item}</li>
        ))}
      </ul>
    </div>
  );
}

export default App;
```

In this example:

- The **useEffect** hook fetches data from your FastAPI API when the component is mounted.
- The fetched data is stored in the **items** state, which is then rendered as a list of items in the browser.

Make sure your FastAPI server is running locally on `http://127.0.0.1:8000` and that you have an endpoint returning a list of items.

3. Connecting the Front-end to Your FastAPI API

At this point, your front-end and back-end are running on different ports (React on port 3000 and FastAPI on port 8000). This can create issues due to **CORS (Cross-Origin Resource Sharing)** restrictions, which prevent the front-end from making requests to the back-end.

Enabling CORS in FastAPI

FastAPI has built-in support for handling CORS. To allow requests from your React front-end, you need to enable CORS in your FastAPI app:

```python
from fastapi import FastAPI
from fastapi.middleware.cors import CORSMiddleware

app = FastAPI()

# Allow requests from the React frontend
app.add_middleware(
    CORSMiddleware,
    allow_origins=["http://localhost:3000"],
    allow_credentials=True,
    allow_methods=["*"],
    allow_headers=["*"],
)
```

This allows requests from `http://localhost:3000` (your React front-end) to interact with the FastAPI back-end.

---

4. Deploying the Full-Stack Application

Once your front-end and back-end are working locally, the next step is to deploy them together. You can use **Docker** to containerize both the FastAPI back-end and the React front-end for deployment to a cloud platform.

Creating a Dockerfile for FastAPI

Start by creating a `Dockerfile` for your FastAPI app:

```dockerfile
# Dockerfile for FastAPI
FROM python:3.11-slim

WORKDIR /app

COPY requirements.txt .
RUN pip install -r requirements.txt

COPY . .

CMD ["uvicorn", "main:app", "--host", "0.0.0.0", "--port", "8000"]
```

Creating a Dockerfile for React

Next, create a `Dockerfile` for your React app:

```dockerfile
# Dockerfile for React
FROM node:16

WORKDIR /app

COPY package*.json ./
RUN npm install

COPY . .

RUN npm run build

CMD ["npx", "serve", "-s", "build"]
```

Docker Compose for Full-Stack Deployment

To deploy both the front-end and back-end together, create a `docker-compose.yml` file:

```
version: "3"
services:
  fastapi:
    build: ./backend
    ports:
      - "8000:8000"
    volumes:
      - ./backend:/app
  react:
    build: ./frontend
    ports:
      - "3000:3000"
    volumes:
      - ./frontend:/app
```

With this setup, Docker Compose will build and run both your FastAPI back-end and React front-end, allowing you to deploy them together in a consistent environment.

Deploying to Heroku

For cloud deployment, platforms like **Heroku** make it easy to deploy full-stack applications. Using the Heroku CLI, you can deploy both your FastAPI API and React front-end with a few simple commands:

1. **Create a Heroku app**:
   ```
   heroku create my-fastapi-app
   ```

2. **Push the code to Heroku**:
   ```
   git push heroku main
   ```

Heroku will automatically build your Docker images and deploy your app.

Conclusion: Bridging the Gap Between Front-end and Back-end

By building a front-end for your FastAPI API, you provide users with a more interactive and intuitive experience. Whether you choose to use React, Vue, or server-side rendering with Jinja2, combining a powerful back-end with a modern front-end can make your application stand out.

Connecting the two requires handling CORS, setting up proper API endpoints, and deploying both parts of the stack together. Tools like Docker and platforms like Heroku make deployment seamless, ensuring that your full-stack application is ready for the real world.

Chapter 17: API Versioning and Evolution

As your API grows and evolves, there will inevitably be changes that could break existing integrations. This is where versioning comes into play, ensuring backward compatibility while allowing you to introduce new features and updates. Versioning allows you to maintain multiple versions of your API, so older clients can continue to use the API without disruptions, while new clients can take advantage of the latest functionality.

In this chapter, we'll explore:

1. **The importance of API versioning.**
2. **Different strategies for versioning your API.**
3. **Managing API deprecations and evolution.**
4. **Best practices for versioning.**

---

1. The Importance of API Versioning

Without versioning, every time you make a breaking change to your API, all clients using the previous version could stop working. This can create chaos for your users, especially if they're depending on your API for critical functionality.

API versioning allows you to:

- Introduce new features without breaking existing functionality.
- Gradually phase out old versions while giving users time to migrate.

- Ensure a smooth transition when major changes are necessary.

Without versioning, users might experience unintended errors when their existing requests no longer work as expected. A well-managed versioning strategy ensures that clients can rely on a stable and predictable API, even as it evolves.

---

2. Strategies for Versioning Your API

There are several ways to implement API versioning, each with its own advantages and disadvantages. The most common strategies include:

URL-Based Versioning

One of the most popular approaches is to include the version number in the API's URL path. This makes it clear which version of the API is being used and is simple to implement.

Example:

```
GET /api/v1/items
GET /api/v2/items
```

In this example, `/v1/` represents version 1 of the API, while `/v2/` represents version 2. Users can switch between versions by updating the URL they use.

Pros:

- Easy to implement and understand.
- Version is clearly visible in the URL.

Cons:

- URL can become cluttered with version numbers, especially if multiple versions are maintained.

Header-Based Versioning

In header-based versioning, the version number is specified in the request headers rather than in the URL. This keeps the URL clean and decouples the versioning from the endpoint paths.

Example:

```
GET /api/items
Accept-Version: v1
```

In this example, the client specifies which version of the API to use in the `Accept-Version` header.

Pros:

- Cleaner URLs since versioning is handled in headers.
- Useful for scenarios where you want to serve different versions without changing the URL.

Cons:

- Less intuitive for users, as the versioning is not immediately visible.
- Requires clients to manage headers correctly.

Query Parameter Versioning

Another approach is to specify the version as a query parameter in the URL. This method keeps the main URL structure the same while allowing users to choose a version via the query string.

Example:

```
GET /api/items?version=v1
GET /api/items?version=v2
```

Pros:

- Simple and flexible, as it allows versioning without changing the URL structure.
- Easy to implement.

Cons:

- Can clutter the URL with query parameters.
- Not as widely used as URL-based or header-based versioning.

---

3. Managing API Deprecation and Evolution

At some point, older versions of your API will need to be deprecated and eventually removed. Deprecation is the process of phasing out an old version of the API while ensuring clients have ample time to migrate to the newer version.

Deprecating an API Version

When deprecating an API version, it's important to communicate clearly with your users. This can be done by:

- **Adding Deprecation Notices**: Include deprecation warnings in the response headers or API documentation to inform users that a version will soon be phased out.
- **Setting a Deprecation Timeline**: Provide a clear timeline for when the old version will no longer be supported, allowing users to prepare for the transition.

Example of a deprecation notice in response headers:

```
Deprecation: true
Deprecation-Date: "2024-01-01"
```

Handling Breaking Changes

Breaking changes are any changes to your API that are not backward-compatible and could cause existing clients to fail. Common examples include:

- Removing or renaming endpoints.
- Changing the structure of the response.
- Introducing new required parameters.

To mitigate the impact of breaking changes, it's essential to maintain support for older versions while guiding users toward the new version. Consider providing clear documentation on the differences between versions and offering migration guides.

Communicating Changes to Users

Effective communication is key when making changes to your API. Always notify users of upcoming changes well in advance and provide detailed information on what has changed, how it affects them, and what they need to do to migrate.

---

4. Best Practices for Versioning

To ensure a smooth versioning process, follow these best practices:

- **Semantic Versioning**: Adopt semantic versioning to signal the nature of changes in your API. For example, increment the major version for breaking changes, the minor version for backward-compatible changes, and the patch version for bug fixes.

- Example: `v1.0.0` -> `v2.0.0` (breaking change), `v1.1.0` (new features, backward-compatible), `v1.0.1` (bug fix).
- **Document Everything**: Always keep your API documentation up-to-date with the latest changes. Clearly document which versions are available, what changes have been made, and how users can transition between versions.
- **Provide Migration Guides**: When releasing a new version with breaking changes, provide clear migration guides to help users update their integrations.
- **Support Multiple Versions Temporarily**: While it's tempting to drop support for old versions immediately, always provide a grace period where multiple versions are supported, allowing users time to migrate.
- **Automate Versioning**: Automate the versioning process as much as possible. Tools like **Swagger/OpenAPI** can help manage versioned APIs, and version control systems (e.g., Git) can help track changes across versions.

Conclusion: Evolving Your API Gracefully

API versioning ensures that your API can grow and evolve without disrupting users who depend on it. By choosing a versioning strategy that fits your needs—whether URL-based, header-based, or query parameter-based—you can maintain backward compatibility while introducing new features and improvements.

Managing API evolution is about more than just version numbers. It's about maintaining a reliable experience for users, communicating changes effectively, and providing the tools and documentation they need to transition smoothly. With a thoughtful versioning strategy in place, your API can evolve gracefully, keeping users happy while embracing the future.

Chapter 18: Performance Benchmarks and Tuning

As your FastAPI application scales and handles increasing traffic, ensuring optimal performance becomes critical. Poor performance can lead to slow response times, unresponsiveness, and even downtime, all of which can negatively impact the user experience. In this chapter, we'll explore how to benchmark your FastAPI application, identify performance bottlenecks, and optimize it for high traffic and low latency.

In this chapter, we'll cover:

1. **Why performance benchmarks matter.**
2. **Tools for benchmarking FastAPI applications.**
3. **Optimizing FastAPI for high traffic.**
4. **Caching for improved performance.**
5. **Asynchronous processing and concurrency.**

---

1. Why Performance Benchmarks Matter

Before optimizing any part of your application, it's important to understand how it performs under different workloads. Benchmarks help you measure key performance metrics like:

- **Request throughput**: The number of requests your API can handle per second.
- **Latency**: The time it takes for your API to respond to a request.

- **Error rates**: The percentage of requests that result in an error.

By identifying bottlenecks through benchmarking, you can make informed decisions about where to focus your optimization efforts, ensuring that improvements are targeted and effective.

---

2. Tools for Benchmarking FastAPI Applications

To accurately measure your API's performance, you'll need to use benchmarking tools that simulate real-world traffic. Here are some popular tools for benchmarking FastAPI applications:

Locust

Locust is a powerful tool for load testing and benchmarking. It allows you to simulate thousands of users making requests to your API and provides detailed metrics on response times, throughput, and error rates.

Here's how to set up a basic Locust test for a FastAPI endpoint:

1. Install Locust:

   ```
   pip install locust
   ```

2. Create a `locustfile.py` to define your load test:

   ```python
   from locust import HttpUser, task

   class APIUser(HttpUser):
       @task
       def get_items(self):
           self.client.get("/items")
   ```

3. Run the Locust load test:

   ```
   locust -f locustfile.py
   ```

Navigate to `http://localhost:8089` to start the test and configure the number of users and request rates. Locust will generate real-time metrics on request performance, helping you identify bottlenecks.

Apache Benchmark (ab)

Another lightweight option for benchmarking is **Apache Benchmark (ab)**. It allows you to quickly test the performance of a single API endpoint. For example, you can run a load test with 1000 requests:

```bash
ab -n 1000 -c 10 http://127.0.0.1:8000/items
```

This command sends 1000 requests to `/items` with 10 concurrent users, providing metrics on average response times, throughput, and the number of failed requests.

wrk

wrk is a high-performance HTTP benchmarking tool that generates a significant amount of load. It's useful for simulating large-scale traffic on your API.

Example command to run `wrk` against your FastAPI app:

```
wrk -t12 -c400 -d30s http://127.0.0.1:8000/items
```

This command runs the benchmark for 30 seconds with 12 threads and 400 concurrent connections, simulating high traffic and collecting detailed metrics.

3. Optimizing FastAPI for High Traffic

Once you've established baseline performance metrics, you can focus on optimizing your FastAPI application for high traffic. Below are several optimization techniques to improve performance:

1. Use Uvicorn with Gunicorn

In production, FastAPI should be run with **Gunicorn** using **Uvicorn workers**. Gunicorn allows you to run multiple worker processes in parallel, improving the API's ability to handle concurrent requests.

```
gunicorn -w 4 -k uvicorn.workers.UvicornWorker main:app
```

This command runs FastAPI with 4 worker processes, ensuring that multiple requests can be handled simultaneously.

2. Optimize Database Queries

Database queries can be a major source of performance bottlenecks. To optimize queries:

- **Use indexes**: Ensure that frequently queried columns are indexed.
- **Limit the amount of data retrieved**: Avoid querying unnecessary fields or records.
- **Use lazy loading**: Load related records only when they are needed, rather than loading them upfront.

```python
Copy code
# Example of selecting specific fields
items = db.query(Item.name, Item.price).filter(Item.category == "Books").all()
```

3. Enable Connection Pooling

Connection pooling reduces the overhead of establishing a new database connection for every request. SQLAlchemy's connection pooling ensures that connections are reused across requests, improving performance.

Here's how to enable connection pooling in SQLAlchemy:

```python
from sqlalchemy import create_engine

engine = create_engine(
    "sqlite:///./test.db",
    pool_size=20,      # Set the connection pool size
    max_overflow=0     # Limit the number of overflow connections
)
```

---

4. Caching for Improved Performance

Caching is one of the most effective ways to improve API performance by reducing the need to process the same requests repeatedly. There are several caching strategies you can use with FastAPI:

In-Memory Caching with Redis

Redis is a high-performance in-memory data store that can be used to cache frequently accessed data. By caching responses in Redis, you can avoid repeated database queries and speed up response times.

Here's an example of using Redis to cache API responses:

```python
import redis

r = redis.Redis()
```

```
@app.get("/items")
def get_items():
    cached_items = r.get("items")
    if cached_items:
        return cached_items
    items = db.query(Item).all()
    r.set("items", items, ex=60)  # Cache items for 60 seconds
    return items
```

In this example, the `/items` response is cached in Redis for 60 seconds, reducing the need for repeated database queries.

Client-Side Caching

Client-side caching can also be enabled using HTTP headers like `Cache-Control`. This instructs the client (e.g., a browser or API consumer) to cache the response for a specified amount of time.

```
@app.get("/items", response_class=JSONResponse)
def get_items():
    response = JSONResponse(content={"items": ["item1", "item2"]})
    response.headers["Cache-Control"] = "public, max-age=3600"
    return response
```

In this example, the client is instructed to cache the response for 1 hour, reducing the number of requests sent to the server.

---

5. Asynchronous Processing and Concurrency

FastAPI's asynchronous nature allows you to handle many requests concurrently, improving throughput without blocking I/O operations. By using **async def** and asynchronous libraries (e.g., for database queries, HTTP requests), you can maximize the performance benefits of FastAPI.

Handling Asynchronous Requests

Here's an example of handling asynchronous requests in FastAPI:

```python
@app.get("/async-items")
async def get_async_items():
    items = await db.fetch_all("SELECT * FROM items")
# Example of async database call
    return items
```

In this example, the database query is run asynchronously, allowing other tasks to be processed in parallel while waiting for the database response.

Concurrency Limits

When dealing with long-running tasks, you may want to limit the number of concurrent requests to avoid overwhelming the server. FastAPI allows you to use **asyncio.Semaphore** to control concurrency:

```python
import asyncio

semaphore = asyncio.Semaphore(10)  # Limit to 10 concurrent requests

@app.get("/limited-items")
async def get_limited_items():
    async with semaphore:
        items = await db.fetch_all("SELECT * FROM items")
        return items
```

In this example, only 10 requests will be processed concurrently, while additional requests are queued.

Conclusion: Tuning Your API for Maximum Performance

Performance tuning is an ongoing process that requires continuous benchmarking, analysis, and optimization. By using tools like Locust and wrk to benchmark your API, you can identify bottlenecks and implement targeted optimizations like connection pooling, caching, and asynchronous processing.

FastAPI's asynchronous capabilities, combined with efficient database queries and caching strategies, allow you to scale your API to handle large volumes of traffic without sacrificing performance. Whether you're optimizing for low latency or high throughput, performance tuning ensures that your API runs smoothly in production, providing the best possible experience for your users.

Chapter 19: Building a Python Tool for API Testing

Testing an API manually can be tedious and time-consuming, especially as the complexity of the application grows. To make testing more efficient, you can build a Python-based tool that automates the testing of your FastAPI API. This custom tool can integrate functional, performance, and security tests to ensure that your API is always functioning correctly and securely.

In this chapter, we'll walk through building a simple API testing tool using Python, leveraging powerful libraries such as **pytest**, **requests**, and **locust**.

---

1. Setting Up the Testing Tool

We'll build a Python tool that:

- Sends API requests and validates responses.
- Tests for performance and scalability.
- Includes security tests (e.g., fuzzing and input validation).

Start by creating a Python script or package that will house the testing logic. Let's break the tool into modules: **functional tests**, **performance tests**, and **security tests**.

Create the directory structure for your testing tool:

```
api_test_tool/
├── functional_tests.py
├── performance_tests.py
├── security_tests.py
```

```
├── utils.py
├── config.py
└── __init__.py
```

The **functional_tests.py** will contain functional tests for the API, **performance_tests.py** for load and performance testing, and **security_tests.py** for basic security checks.

---

2. Functional Testing with pytest and requests

pytest is a popular testing framework for Python, and **requests** is a powerful library for making HTTP requests. By combining these two libraries, we can automate testing API endpoints to verify that they behave as expected.

Here's an example of a functional test for a FastAPI endpoint:

```python
import requests
import pytest

BASE_URL = "http://127.0.0.1:8000"

def test_get_items():
    response = requests.get(f"{BASE_URL}/items")
    assert response.status_code == 200
    assert "items" in response.json()

def test_create_item():
    payload = {"name": "Book", "price": 10.99}
    response = requests.post(f"{BASE_URL}/items", json=payload)
    assert response.status_code == 201
    assert response.json()["name"] == "Book"
```

This test tool uses **pytest** to run functional tests and checks that the API endpoints return the correct status codes and data.

3. Performance Testing with Locust

To ensure your API can handle a high load, we can integrate **Locust** into our tool to simulate concurrent users making requests to the API. Locust allows us to define user behavior and measure the performance of the API under stress.

Here's how you can write a performance test using Locust:

```python
from locust import HttpUser, task, between

class APIPerformanceTest(HttpUser):
    wait_time = between(1, 5)

    @task
    def get_items(self):
        self.client.get("/items")

    @task
    def create_item(self):
        self.client.post("/items", json={"name": "Laptop", "price": 1500})
```

You can run the performance test by using:

```
locust -f performance_tests.py
```

Locust will simulate multiple users interacting with your API and provide real-time statistics on request throughput, latency, and error rates.

---

4. Security Testing

For basic security testing, such as fuzzing and input validation, you can build tests that attempt to send invalid or unexpected data to the API and observe how it responds.

Here's a basic example of a security test:

```python
import requests

def test_fuzzing():
    fuzz_data = ["", "<script>alert(1)</script>", "DROP TABLE users;", "1234567890" * 1000]
    for data in fuzz_data:
        response = requests.post(f"{BASE_URL}/items", json={"name": data, "price": "abc"})
        assert response.status_code != 500, f"API crashed with input: {data}"
```

This test sends unexpected input to the **/items** endpoint and ensures that the API doesn't crash or behave unpredictably when encountering invalid data.

5. Configuring the Tool

Create a **config.py** file to store configuration variables, such as the API's base URL or the number of simulated users for the performance tests:

```
BASE_URL = "http://127.0.0.1:8000"
NUM_USERS = 100
```

By storing these settings in a separate file, you can easily modify the configuration for different environments (e.g., development, staging, production).

Conclusion: Automating API Testing for Efficiency

By building a Python tool to automate API testing, you can streamline the testing process and ensure that your FastAPI application remains robust, high-performing, and secure. Functional tests validate that each endpoint works as expected, performance tests ensure scalability, and security tests help identify potential vulnerabilities.

This tool can be integrated into your continuous integration (CI) pipeline to automatically run tests whenever you deploy new code, providing peace of mind that your API is in top shape.

Bibliography

1. **Sebastián Ramírez**. *FastAPI Documentation* [online]. Available at: https://fastapi.tiangolo.com/. FastAPI's official documentation, detailing the framework's core features, usage, and best practices.

2. **SQLAlchemy Documentation**. *SQLAlchemy ORM and Core Documentation* [online]. Available at: https://docs.sqlalchemy.org/. Comprehensive guide to using SQLAlchemy as an ORM and working directly with the database using SQL queries.

3. **Pydantic Documentation**. *Data validation and settings management using Python type annotations* [online]. Available at: https://docs.pydantic.dev/. The official documentation for Pydantic, used for data validation in Python.

4. **Uvicorn**. *The lightning-fast ASGI server implementation* [online]. Available at: https://www.uvicorn.org/. Uvicorn's documentation, explaining how to run FastAPI apps in production.

5. **Redis Labs Documentation**. *Redis: The open-source, in-memory data structure store* [online]. Available at: https://redis.io/documentation. Detailed explanation of Redis and how it can be used for caching and message brokering.

6. **OWASP ZAP Documentation**. *OWASP Zed Attack Proxy (ZAP)* [online]. Available at: https://owasp.org/www-project-zap/. Documentation for using ZAP, a tool for penetration testing APIs.

7. **Locust Documentation**. *Load testing with Locust* [online]. Available at: https://locust.io/. Guide on how to use Locust for load testing and benchmarking your API's performance.

8. **Burp Suite**. *Burp Suite Documentation* [online]. Available at: https://portswigger.net/burp. Comprehensive documentation for using Burp Suite in web application and API security testing.

9. **TryHackMe**. *Learn Cybersecurity with TryHackMe* [online]. Available at: https://tryhackme.com/. Online platform for learning and practicing cybersecurity skills through challenges and tutorials.

10. **Hack The Box**. *Hack The Box: Cybersecurity training platform* [online]. Available at: https://www.hackthebox.com/. Platform for hacking challenges and cybersecurity skill development.

11. **pytest Documentation**. *Simple and scalable test automation* [online]. Available at: https://docs.pytest.org/. Detailed guide to using pytest for test automation in Python.

12. **Docker Documentation**. *Docker: Develop and Deploy Containers* [online]. Available at: https://docs.docker.com/. Official Docker documentation for building, deploying, and running containers.

Notes:

www.ingramcontent.com/pod-product-compliance
Lightning Source LLC
Chambersburg PA
CBHW052207220526
45471CB00004B/1850